FILLER

RICK SPEARS
ROB G

AiT★PLANET LAR
SAN FRANCISCO

FILLER
by Rick Spears
and Rob G.

published by
AiT/Planet Lar
2034 47th Avenue
San Francisco, CA
94116

First Edition: March 2005
10 9 8 7 6 5 4 3 2 1

Book design and production
by Rob Blatherwick
and Whiskey Island

ISBN: 1-932051-32-5

Printed and bound in Canada
by Quebecor Printing, inc.

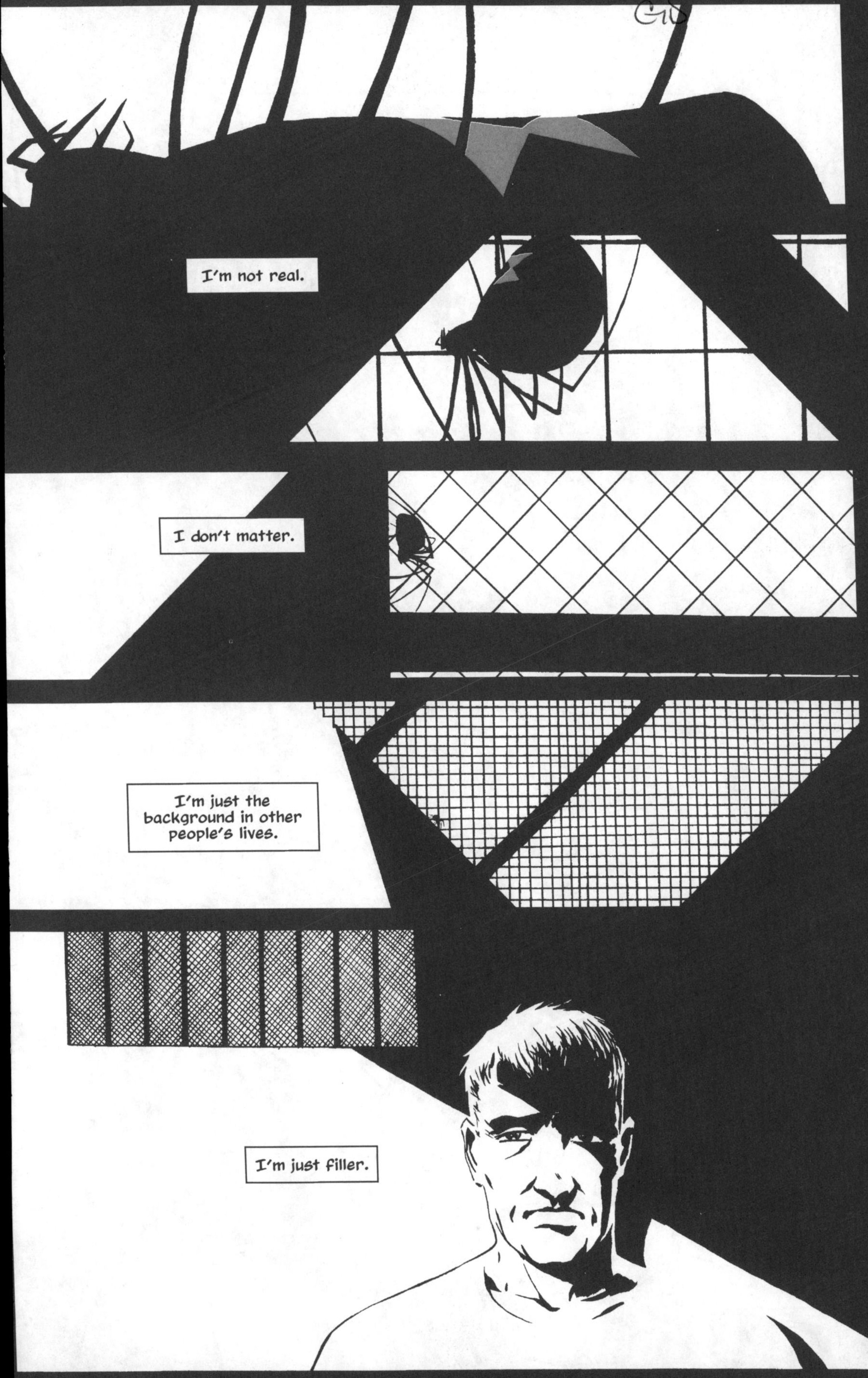
I'm not real.
I don't matter.
I'm just the background in other people's lives.
I'm just filler.

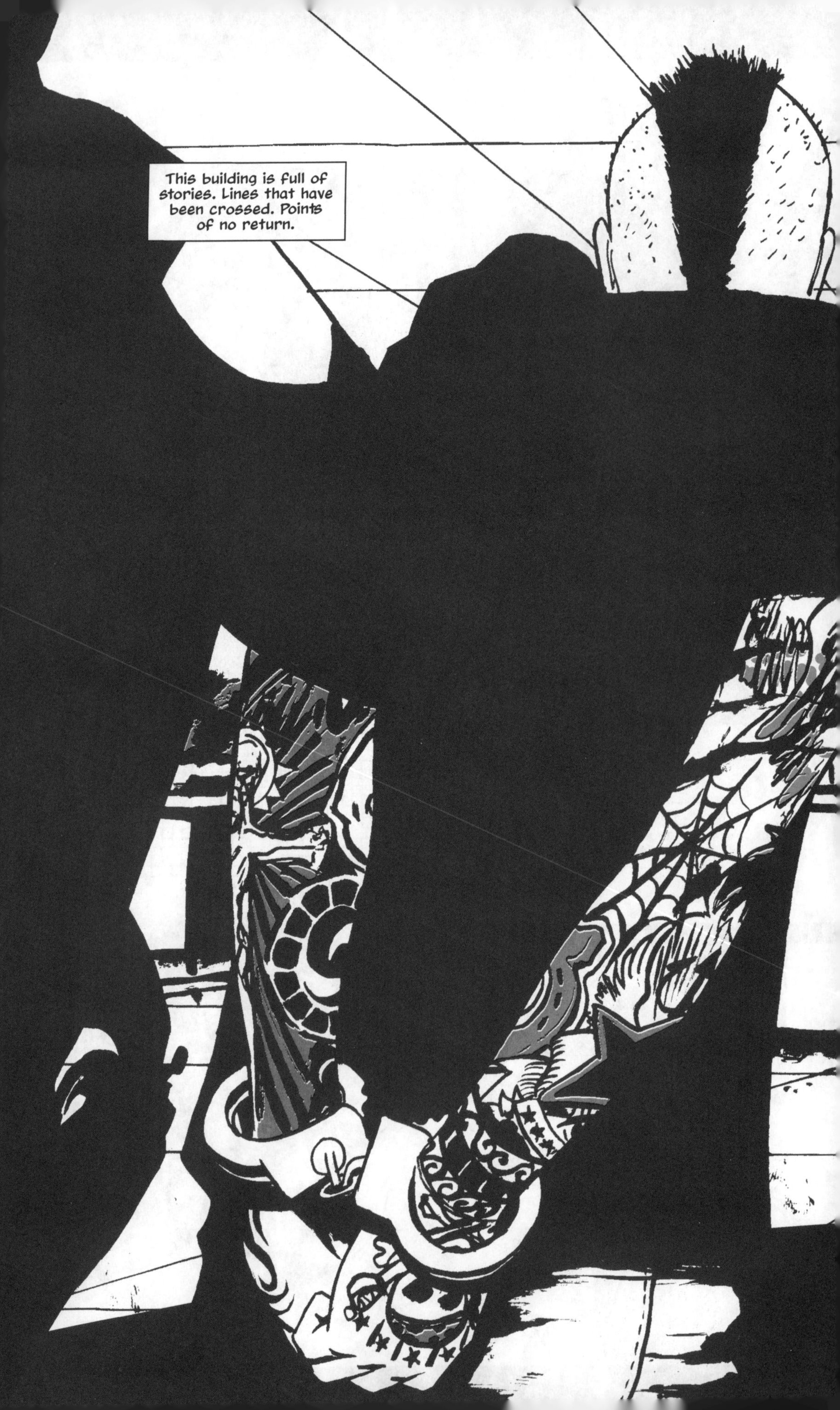
This building is full of stories. Lines that have been crossed. Points of no return.

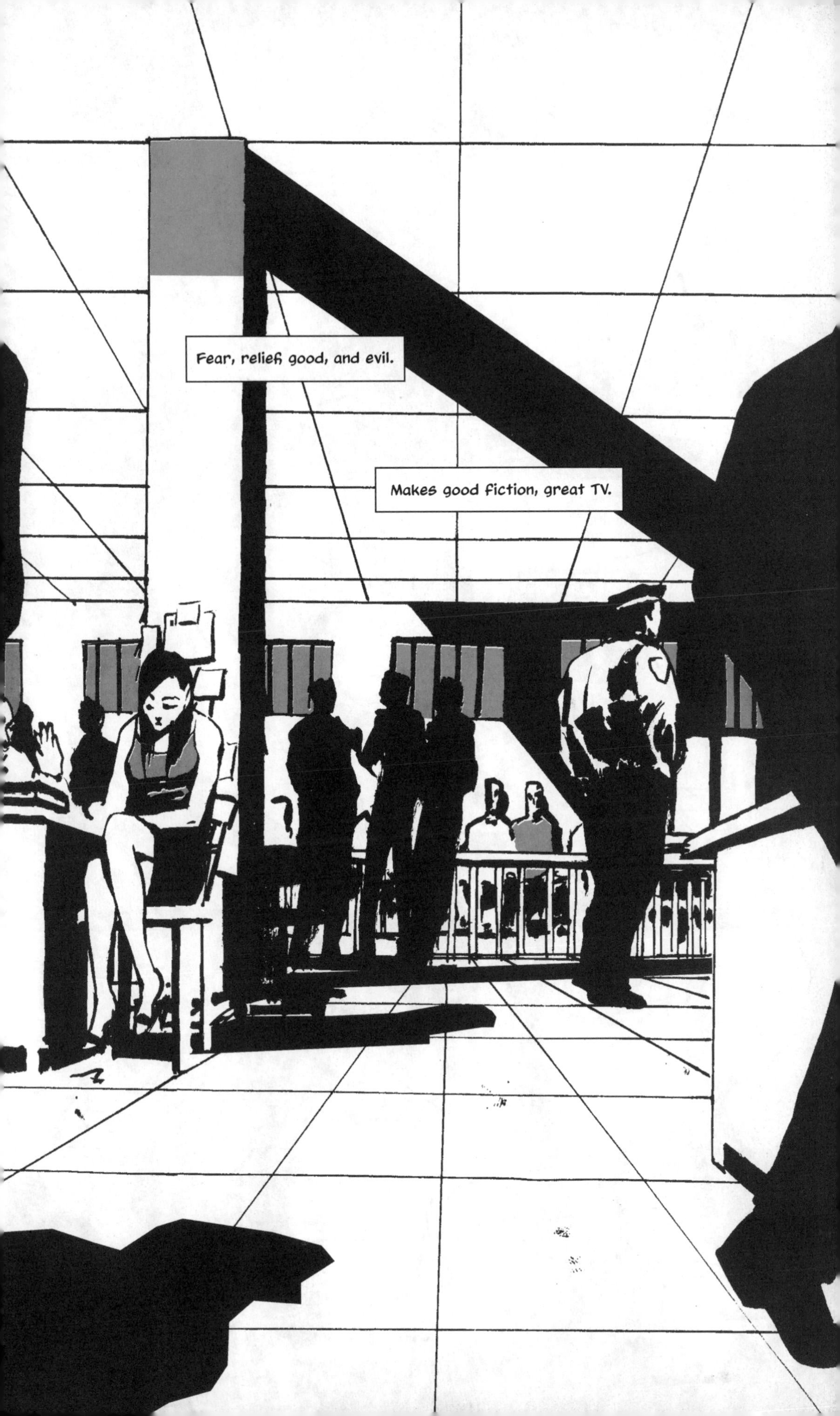
Fear, reliefs good, and evil.
Makes good fiction, great TV.

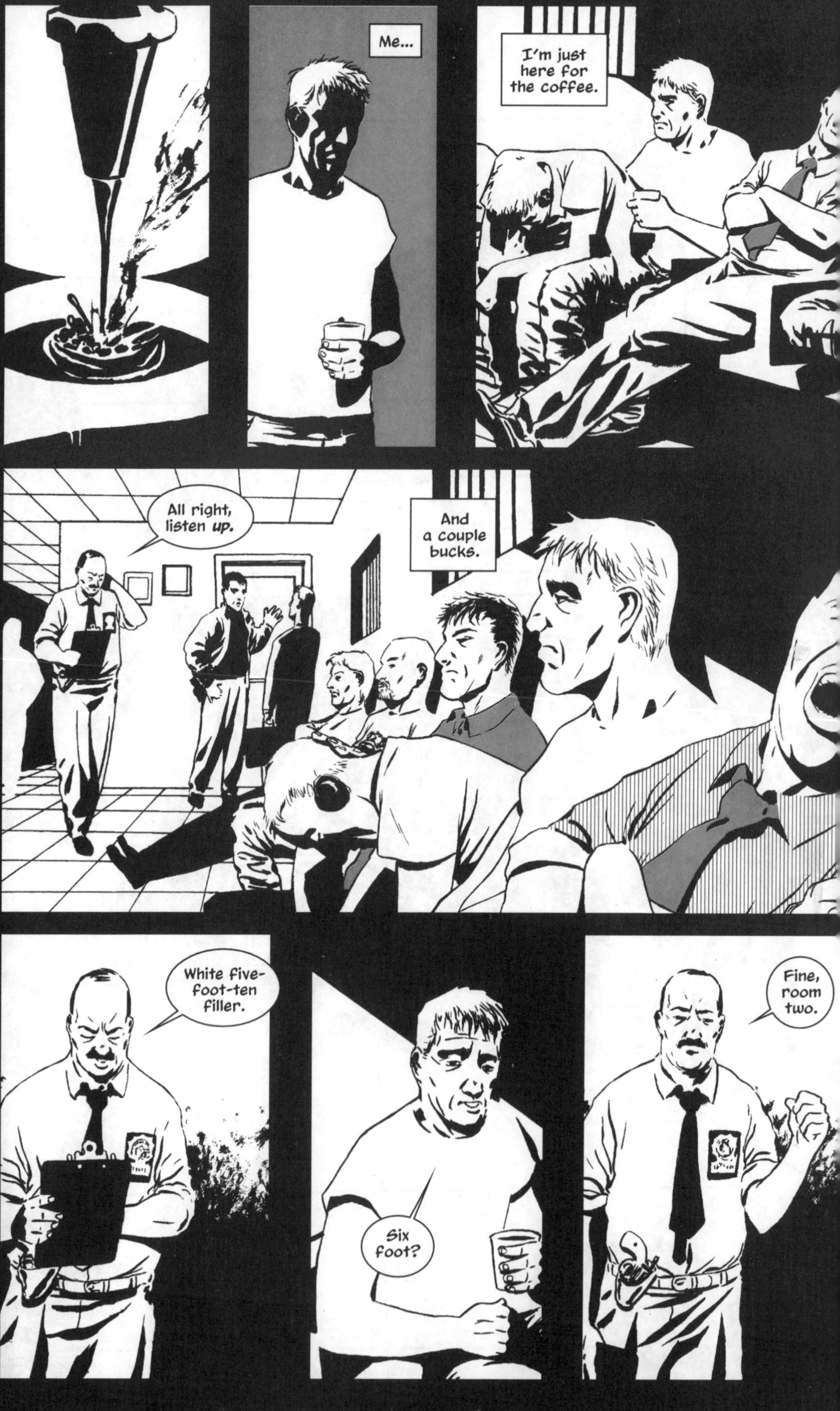

Me...
I'm just here for the coffee.
All right, listen up.
And a couple bucks.
White five-foot-ten filler.
Six foot?
Fine, room two.

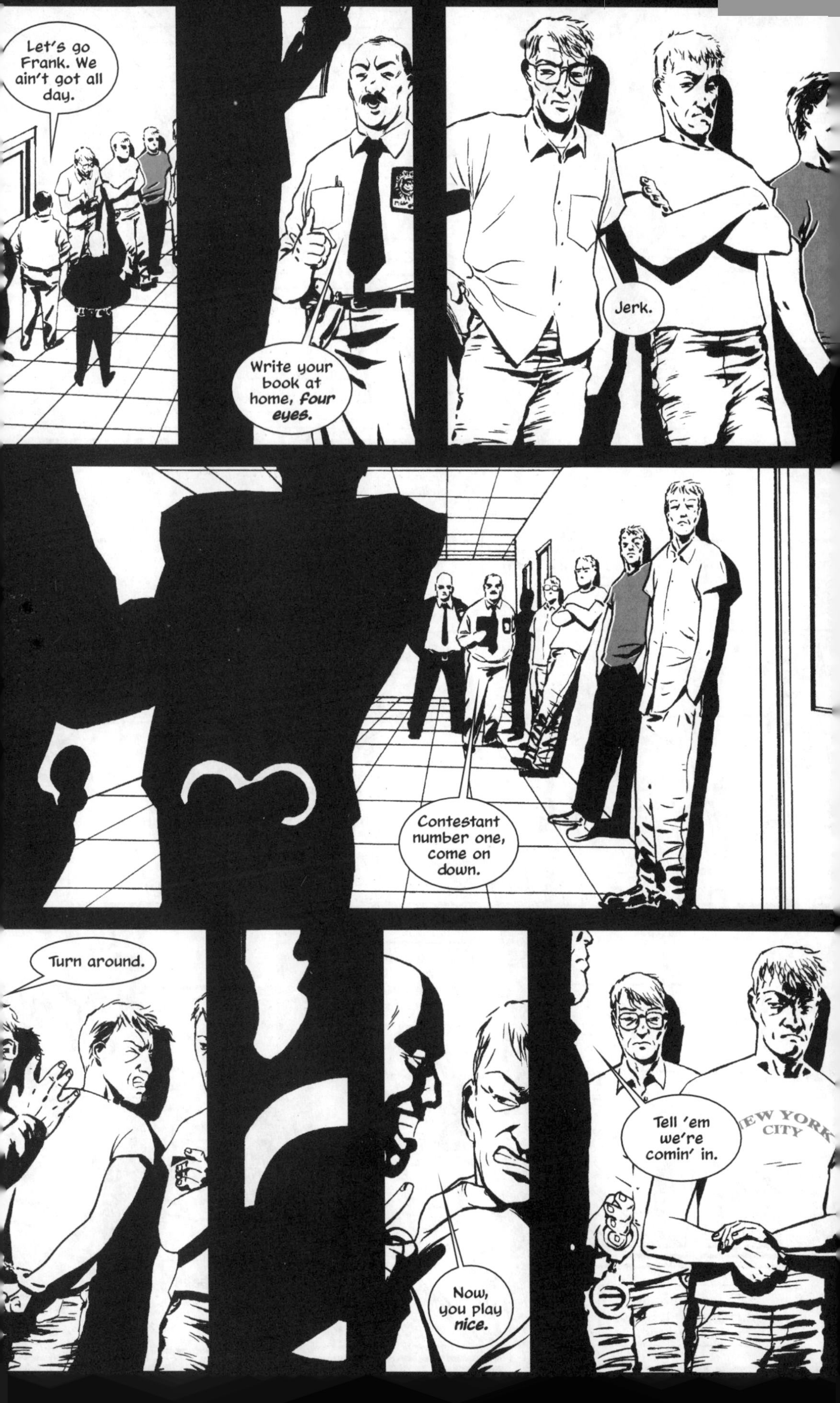
Let's go Frank. We ain't got all day.
Write your book at home, *four eyes.*
Jerk.
Contestant number one, come on down.
Turn around.
Now, you play *nice.*
Tell 'em we're comin' in.
NEW YORK CITY

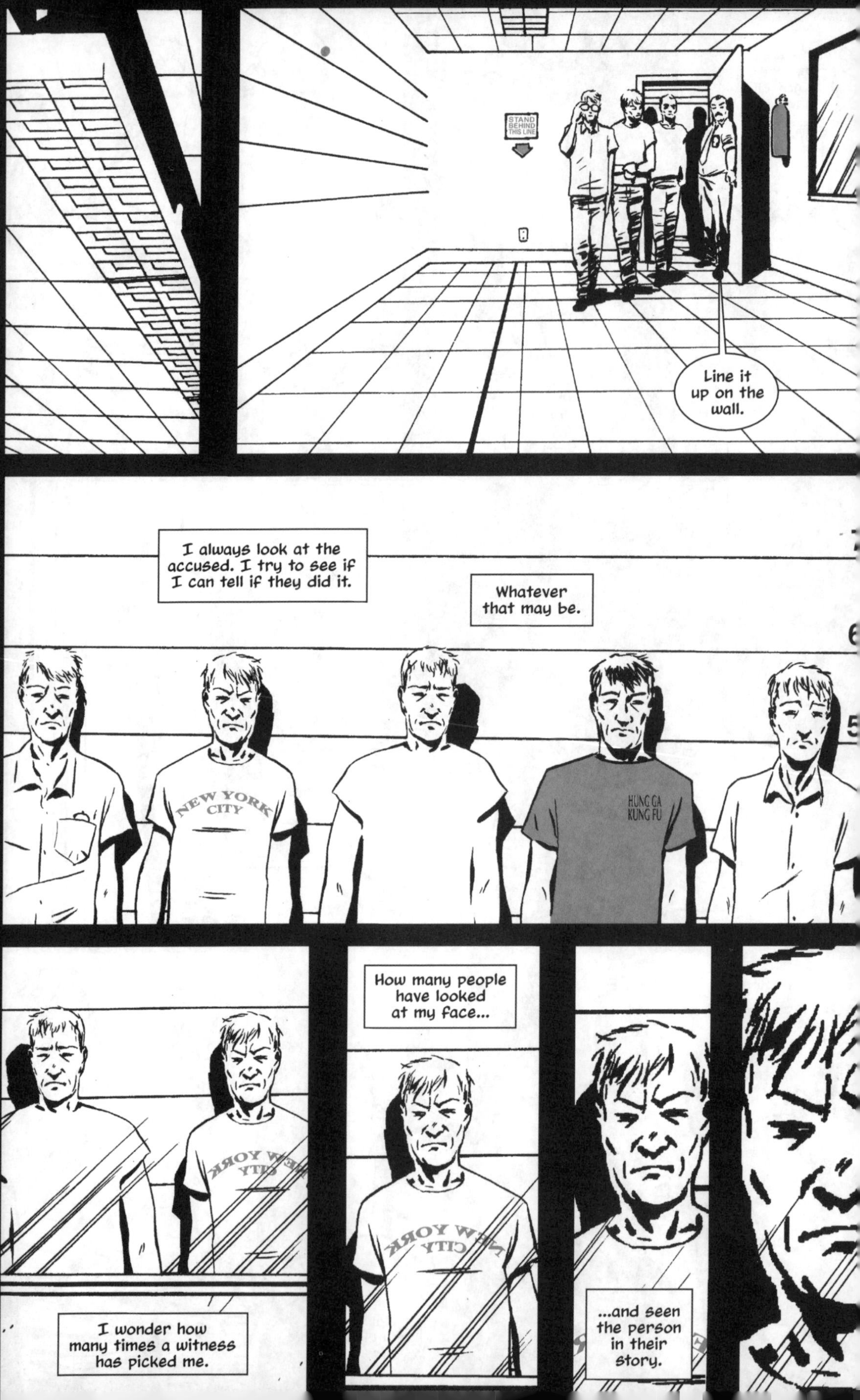

STAND BEHIND THIS LINE
Line it up on the wall.
I always look at the accused. I try to see if I can tell if they did it.
Whatever that may be.
NEW YORK CITY
HUNG GA KUNG FU
I wonder how many times a witness has picked me.
How many people have looked at my face...
...and seen the person in their story.

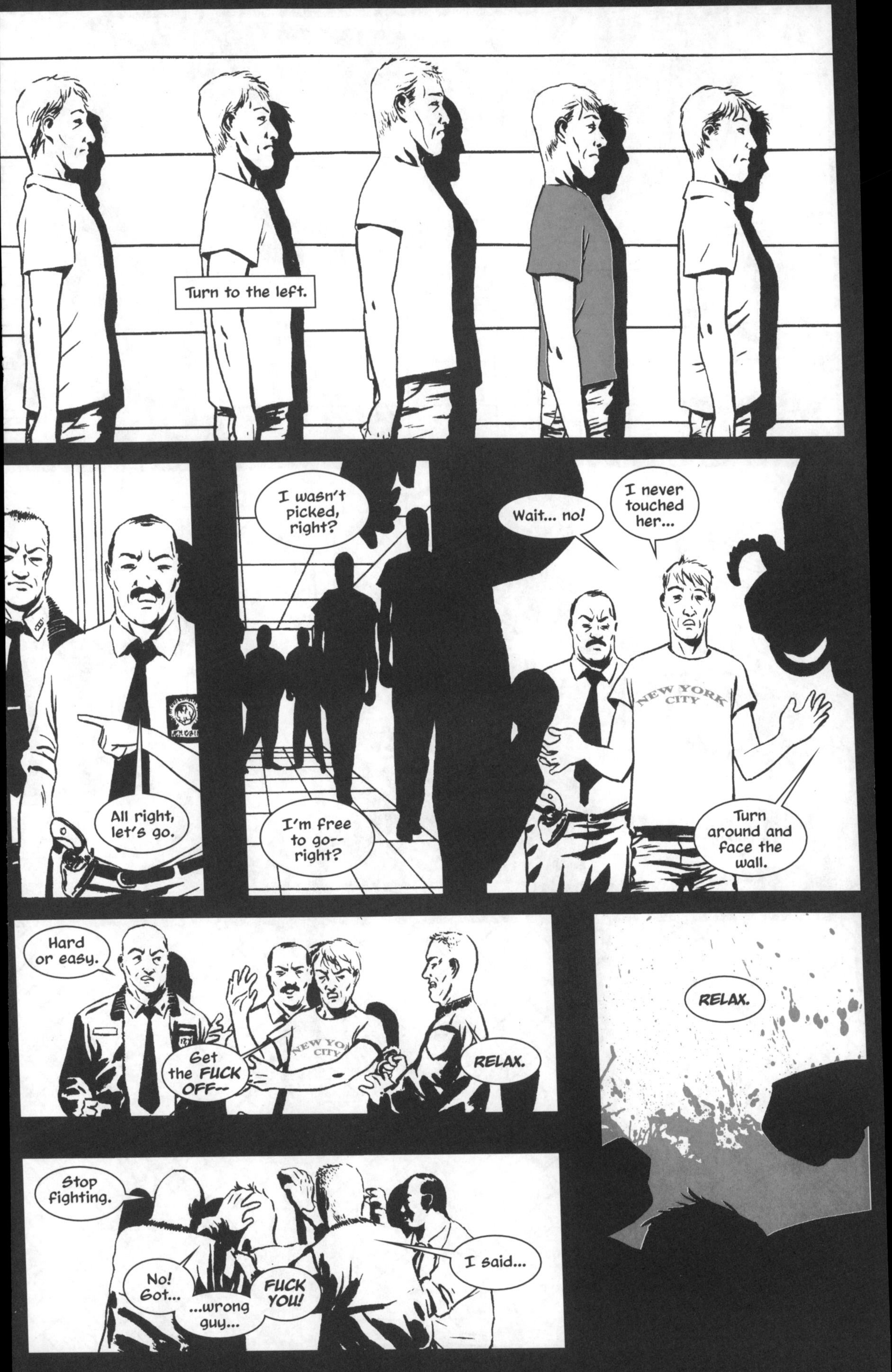
Turn to the left.
All right, let's go.
I wasn't picked, right?
I'm free to go-- right?
Wait... no!
I never touched her...
Turn around and face the wall.
NEW YORK CITY
Hard or easy.
Get the FUCK OFF--
RELAX.
RELAX.
Stop fighting.
No! Got...
...wrong guy...
FUCK YOU!
I said...

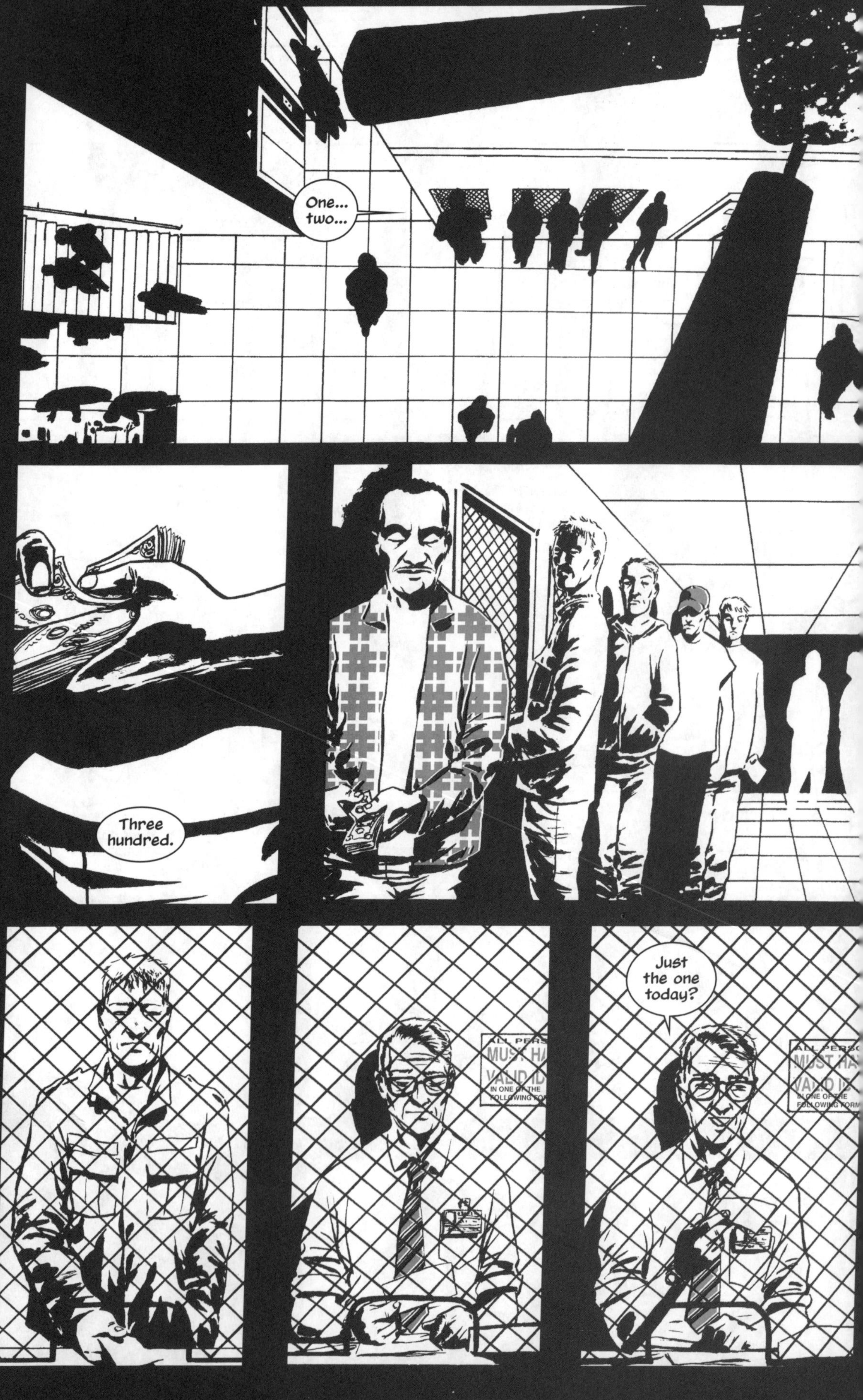
One... two...
Three hundred.
ALL PERSO
MUST HA
VALID ID
IN ONE OF THE FOLLOWING FO
Just the one today?

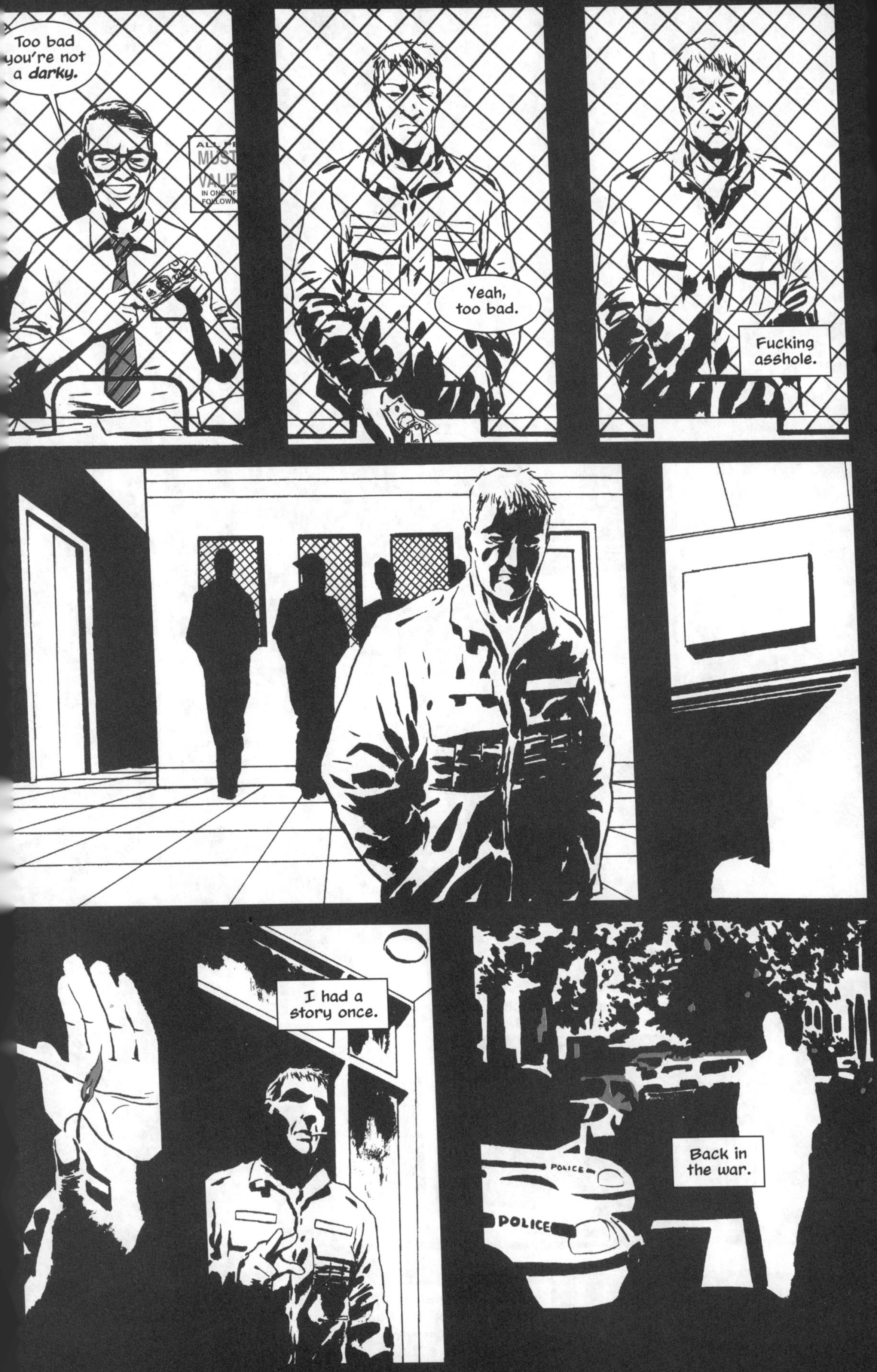
Too bad you're not a *darky.*
Yeah, too bad.
Fucking asshole.
I had a story once.
POLICE
POLICE
Back in the war.

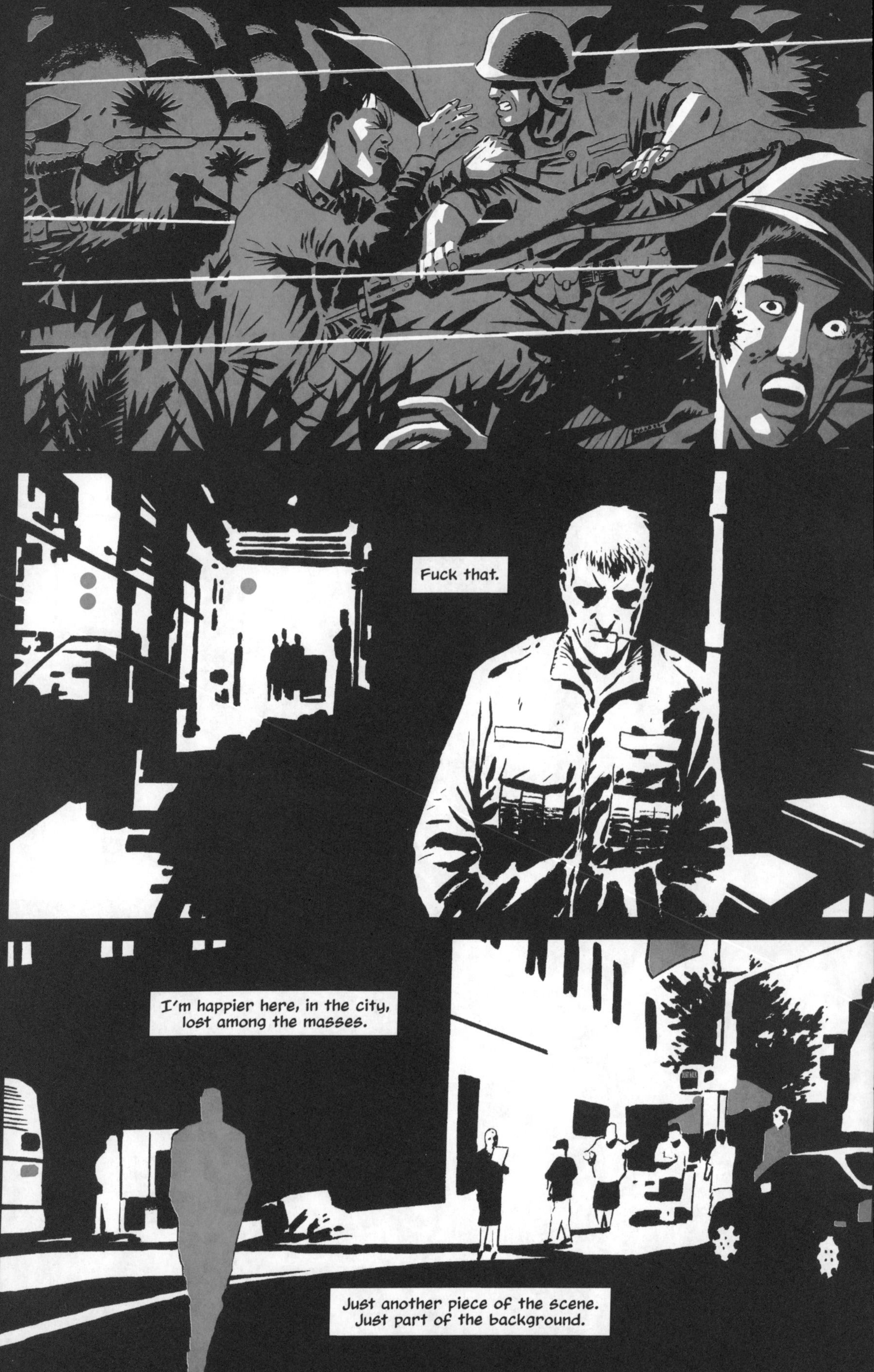
Fuck that.
I'm happier here, in the city, lost among the masses.
Just another piece of the scene. Just part of the background.

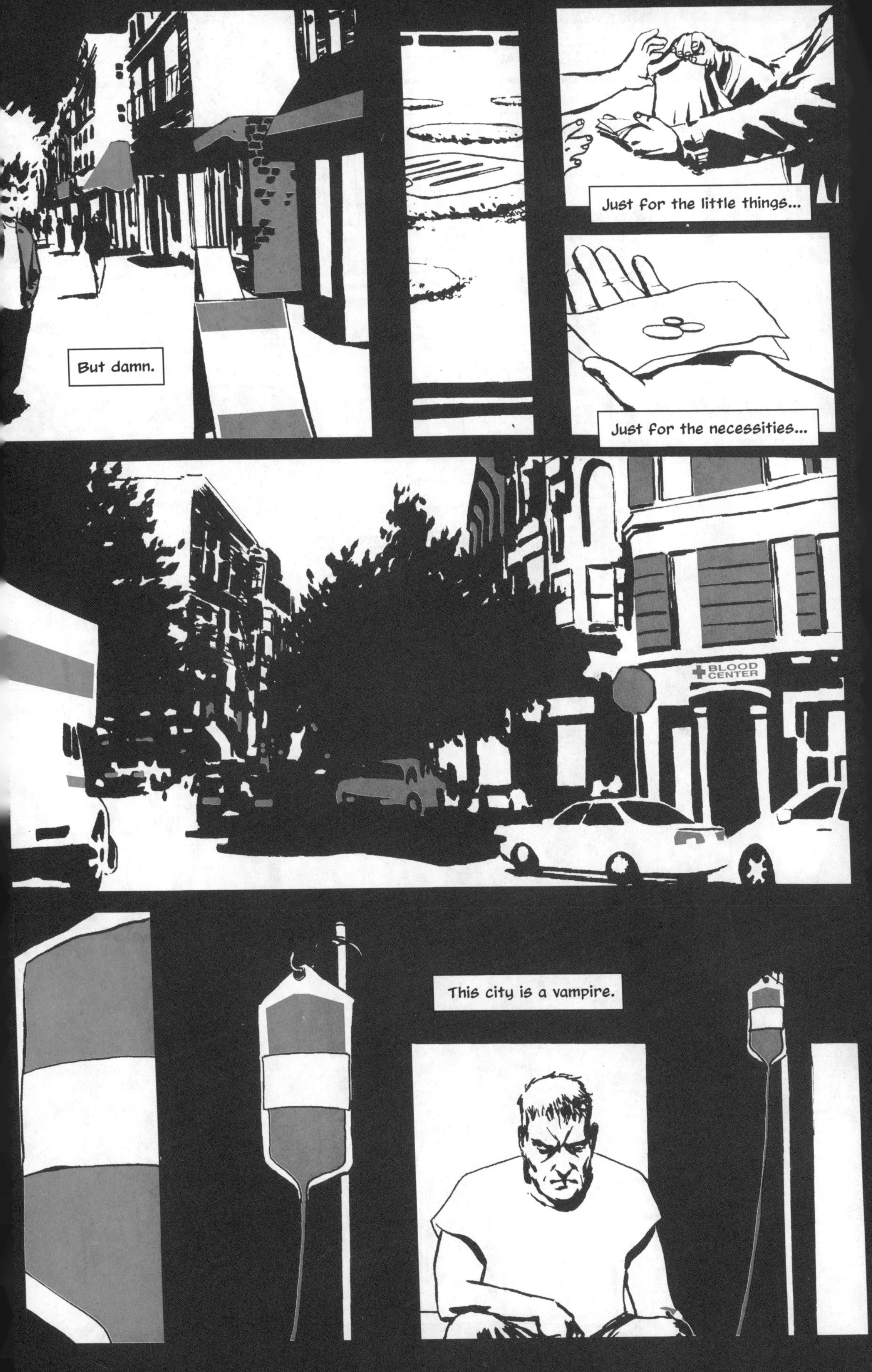
But damn.
Just for the little things...
Just for the necessities...
BLOOD CENTER
This city is a vampire.

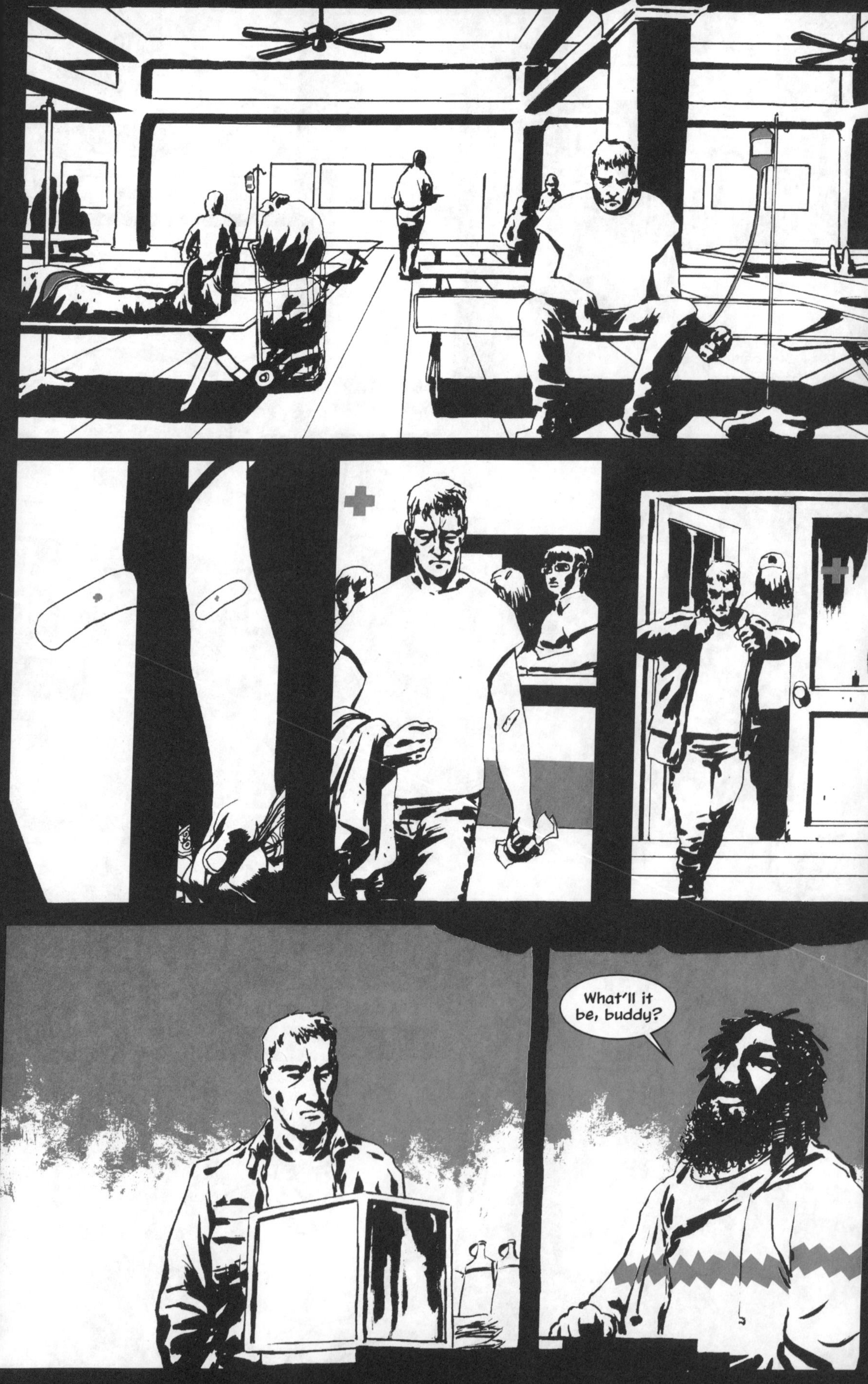
What'll it be, buddy?

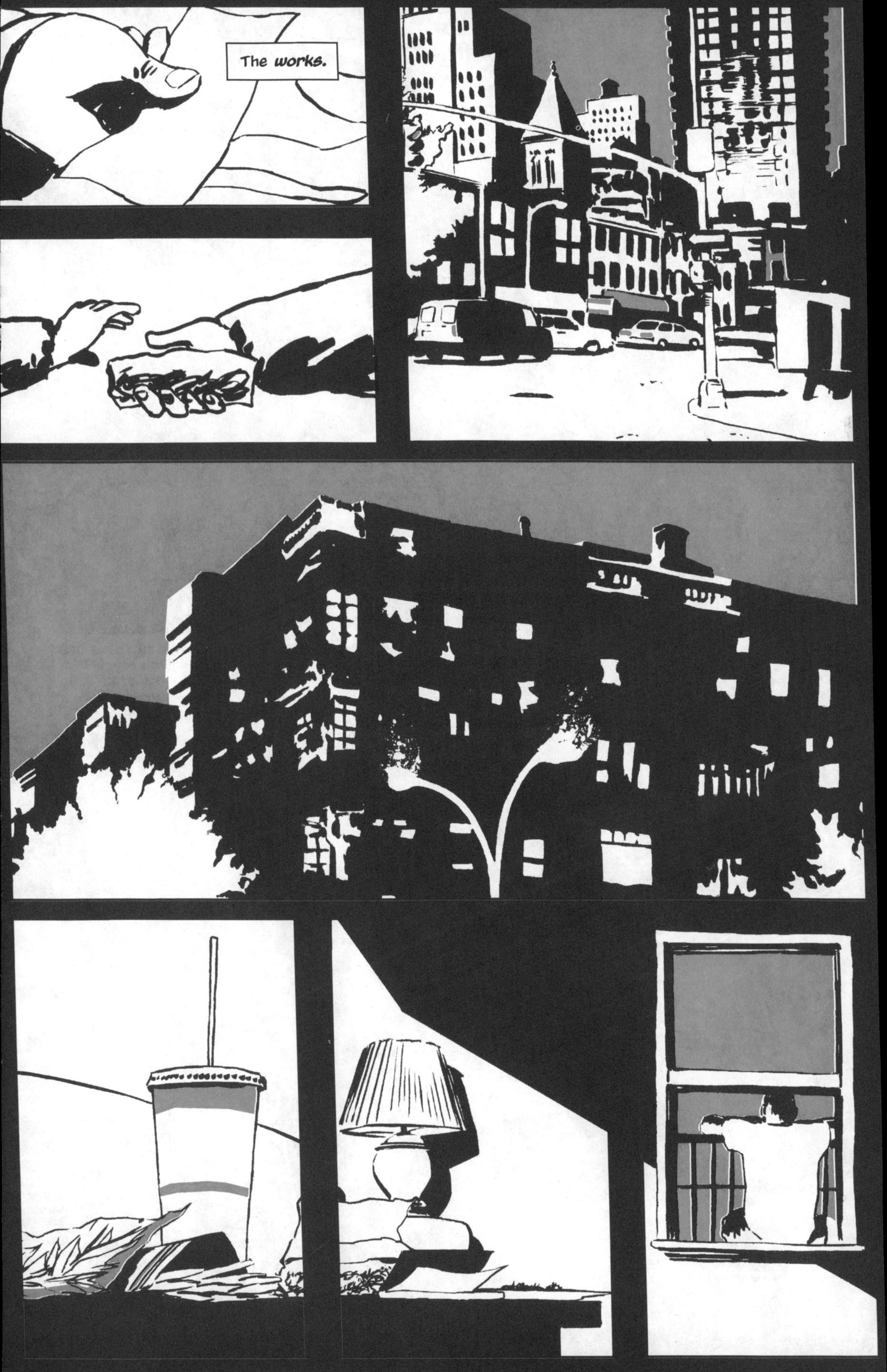
The *works.*

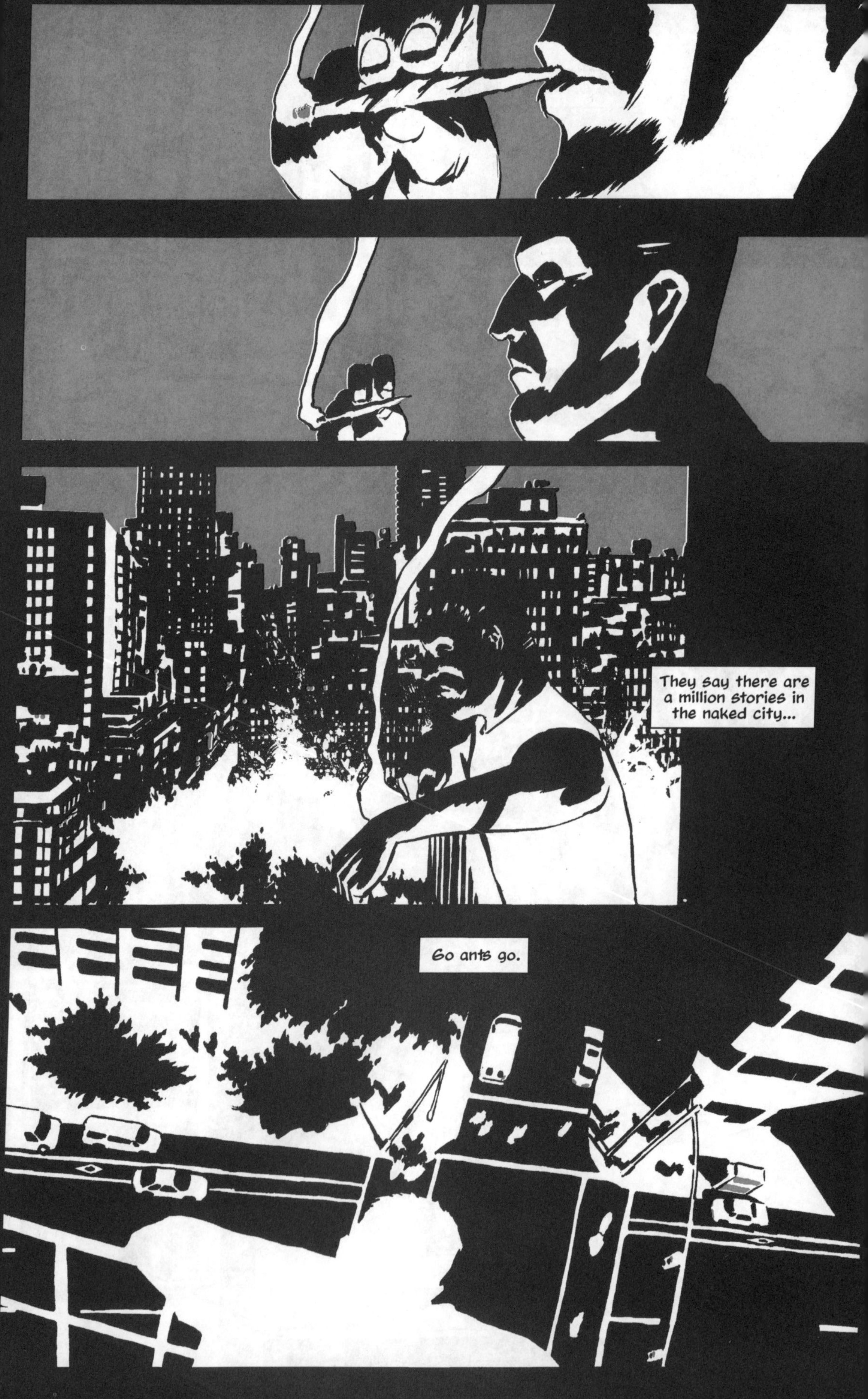
They say there are a million stories in the naked city...
Go ants go.

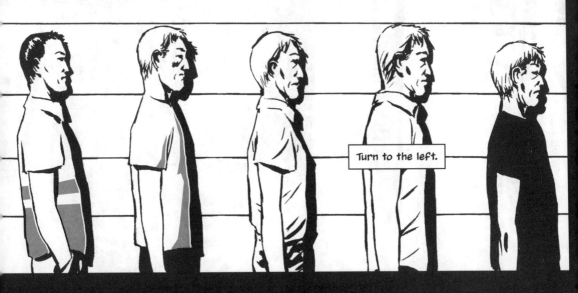

Turn to the left.

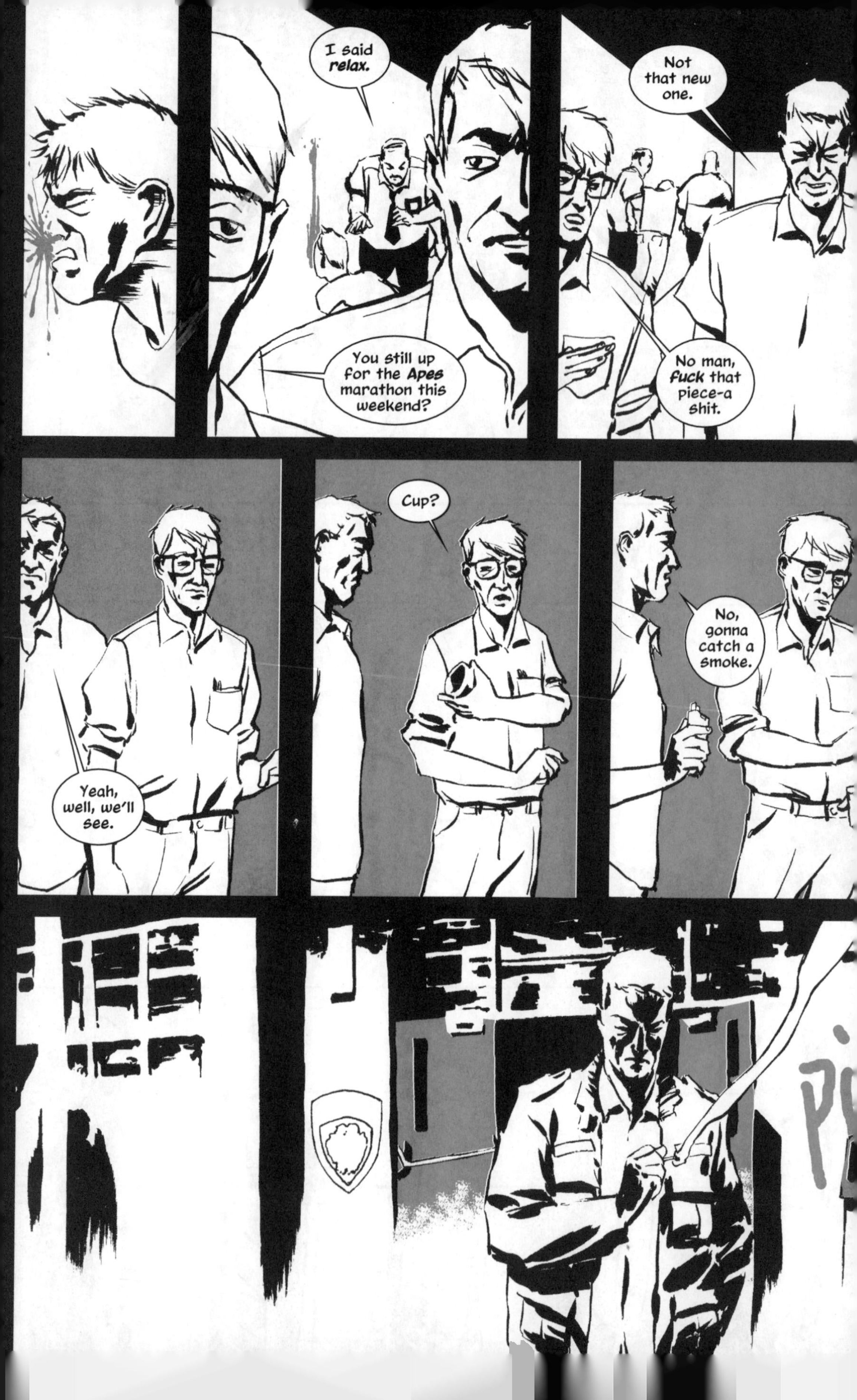

I said relax.
You still up for the Apes marathon this weekend?
Not that new one.
No man, fuck that piece-a shit.
Yeah, well, we'll see.
Cup?
No, gonna catch a smoke.

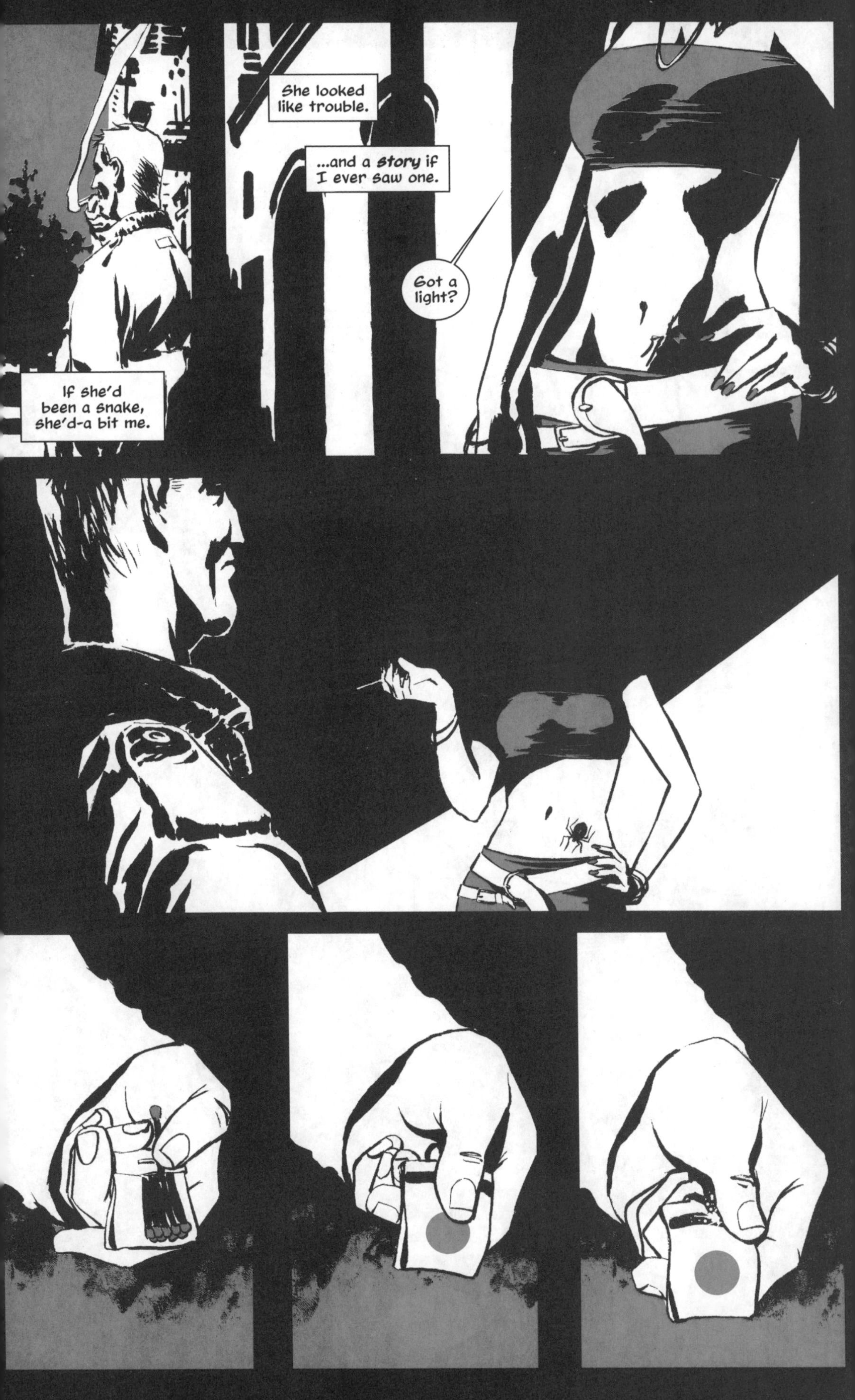
If she'd been a snake, she'd-a bit me.
She looked like trouble.
...and a *story* if I ever saw one.
Got a light?

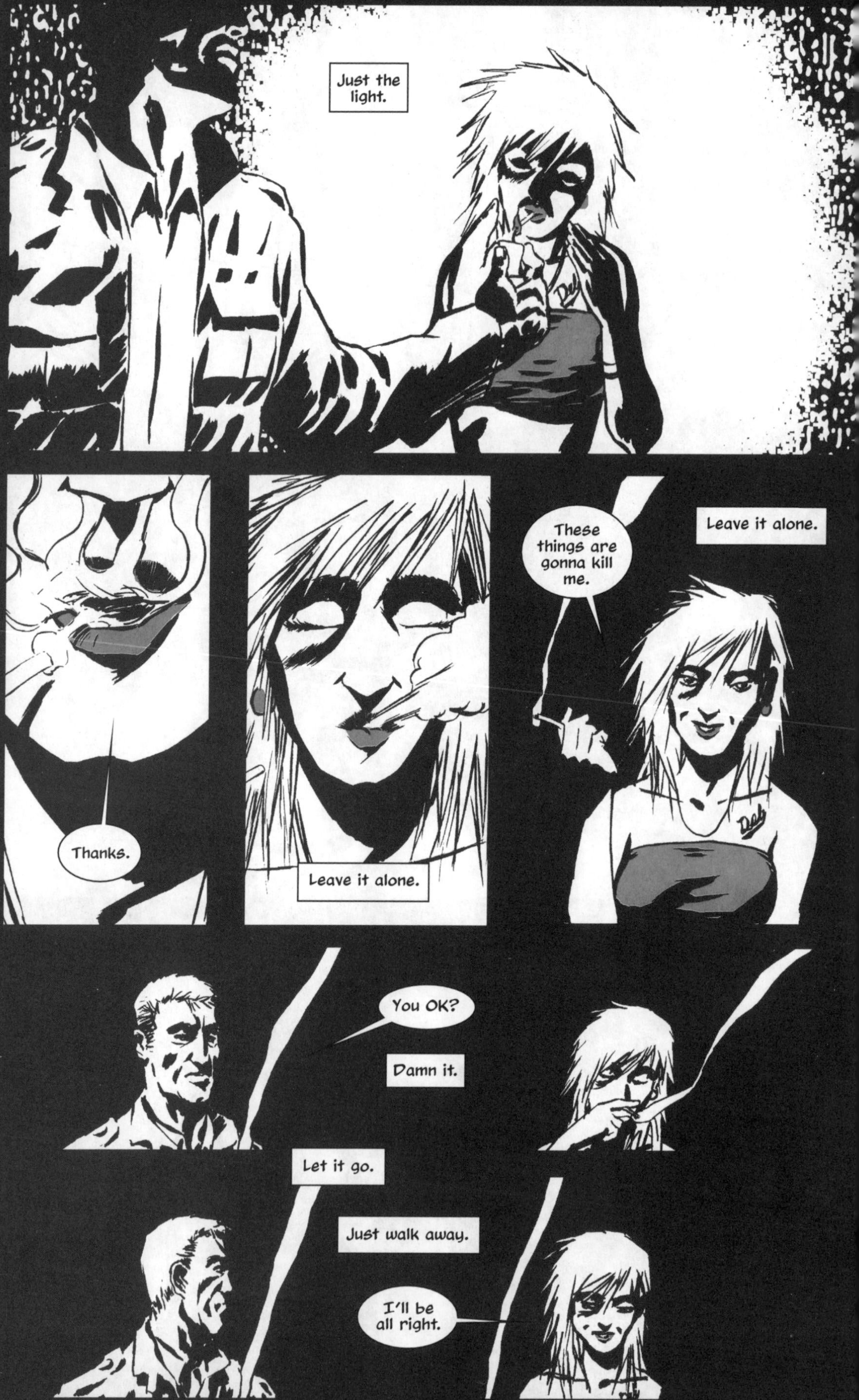
Just the light.
Thanks.
Leave it alone.
These things are gonna kill me.
Leave it alone.
You OK?
Damn it.
Let it go.
Just walk away.
I'll be all right.

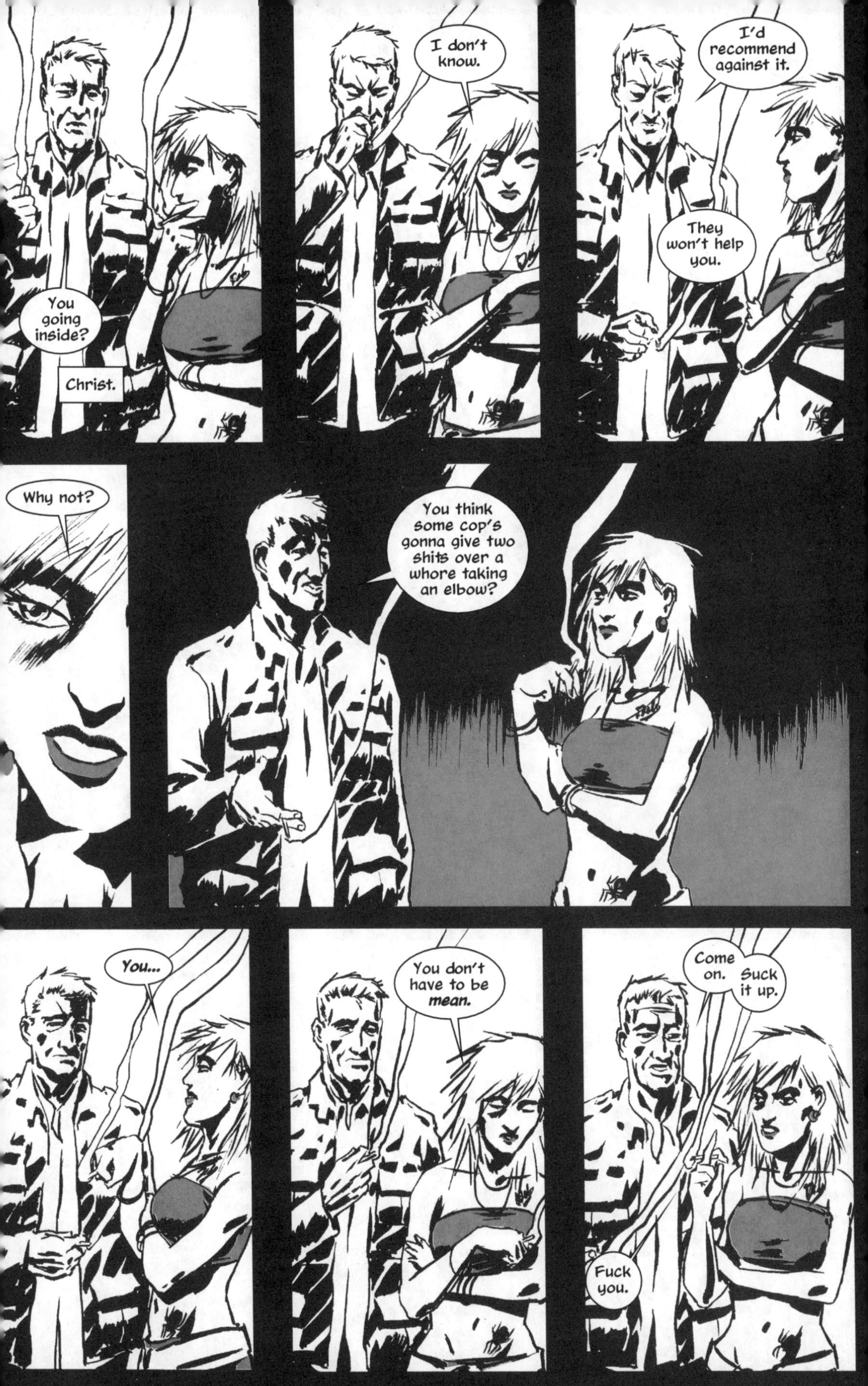
You going inside?
Christ.
I don't know.
I'd recommend against it.
They won't help you.
Why not?
You think some cop's gonna give two shits over a whore taking an elbow?
You...
You don't have to be *mean.*
Come on.
Suck it up.
Fuck you.

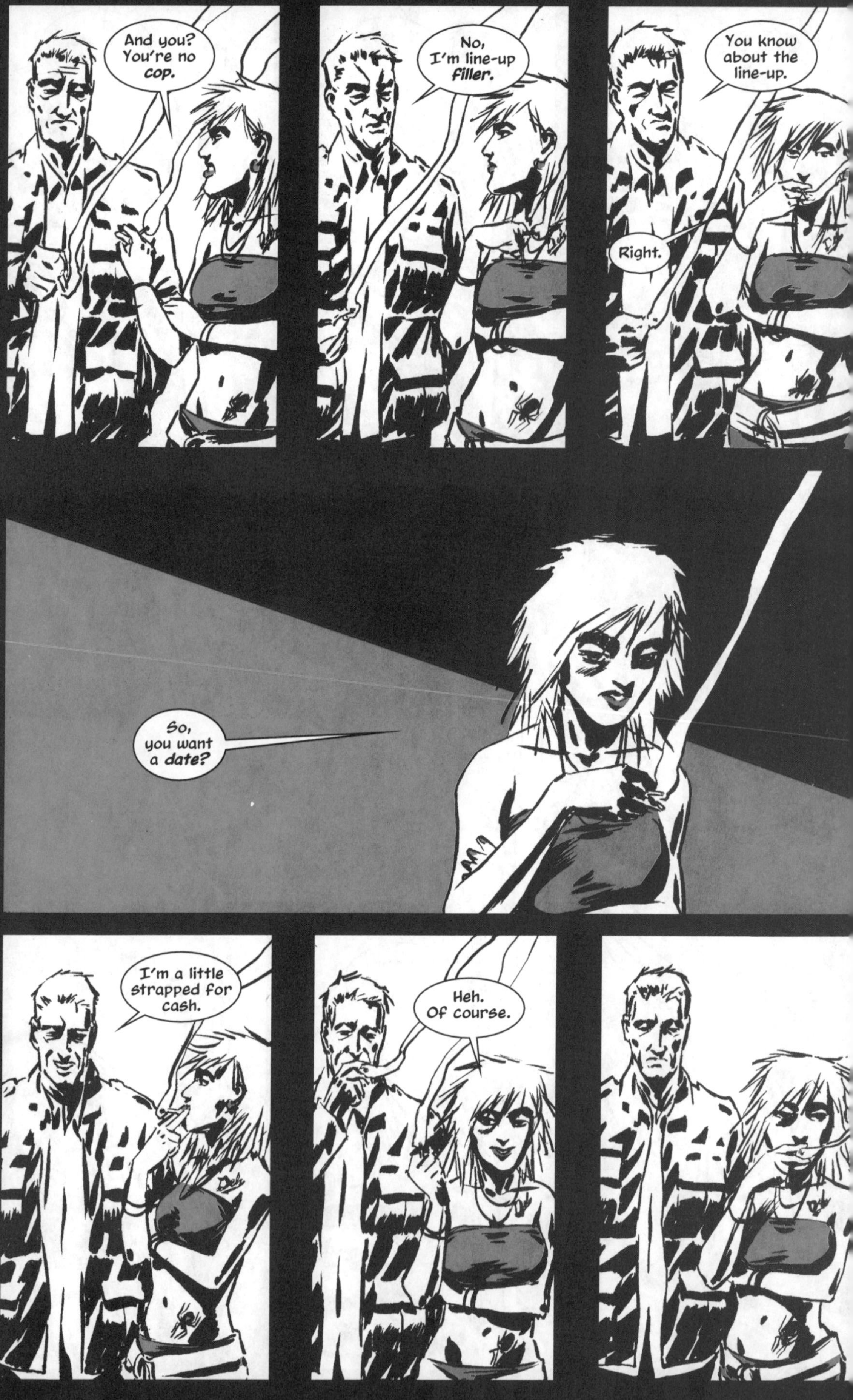
And you? You're no cop.
No, I'm line-up filler.
You know about the line-up.
Right.
So, you want a date?
I'm a little strapped for cash.
Heh. Of course.

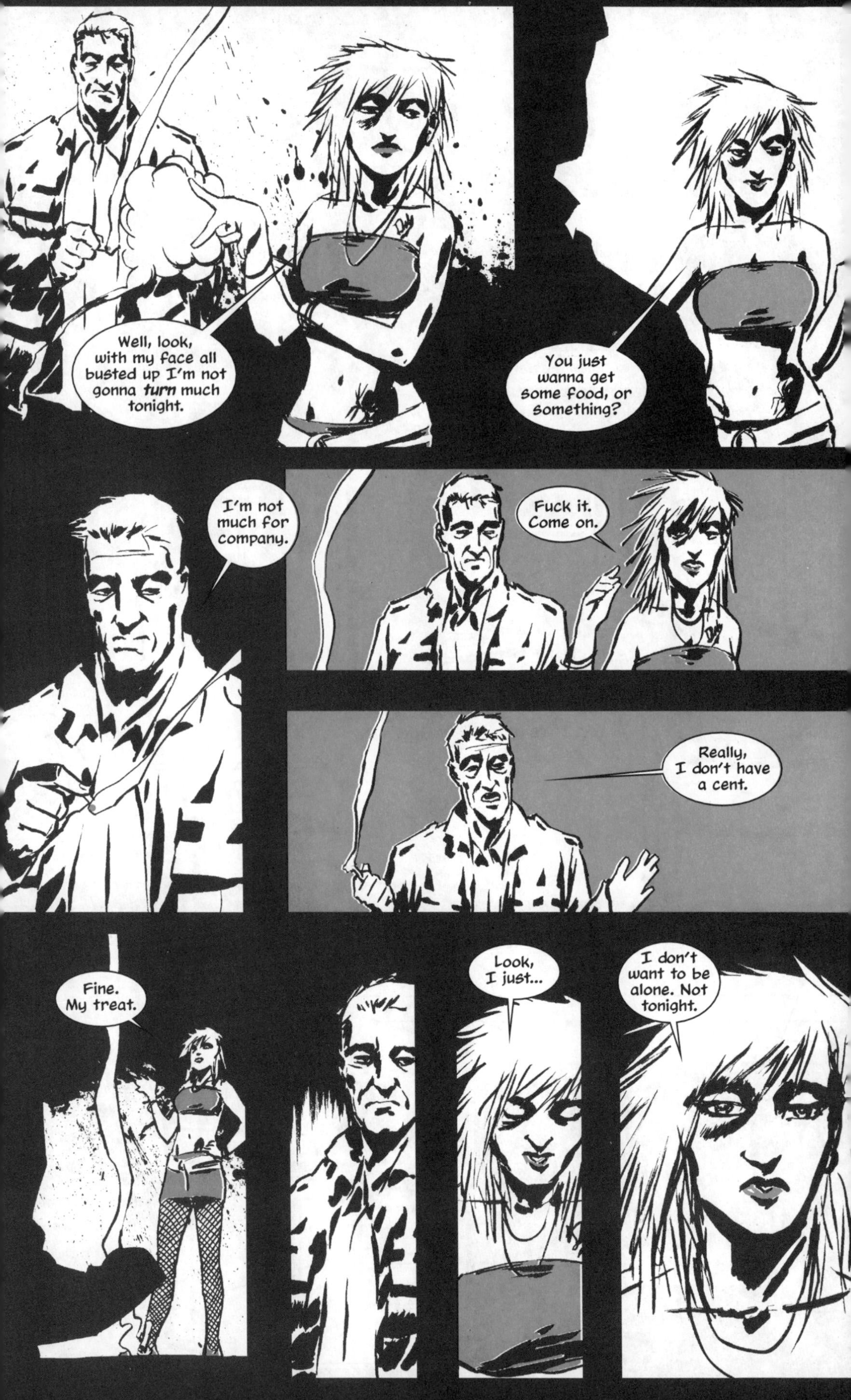
Well, look, with my face all busted up I'm not gonna *turn* much tonight.
You just wanna get some food, or something?
I'm not much for company.
Fuck it. Come on.
Really, I don't have a cent.
Fine. My treat.
Look, I just...
I don't want to be alone. Not tonight.

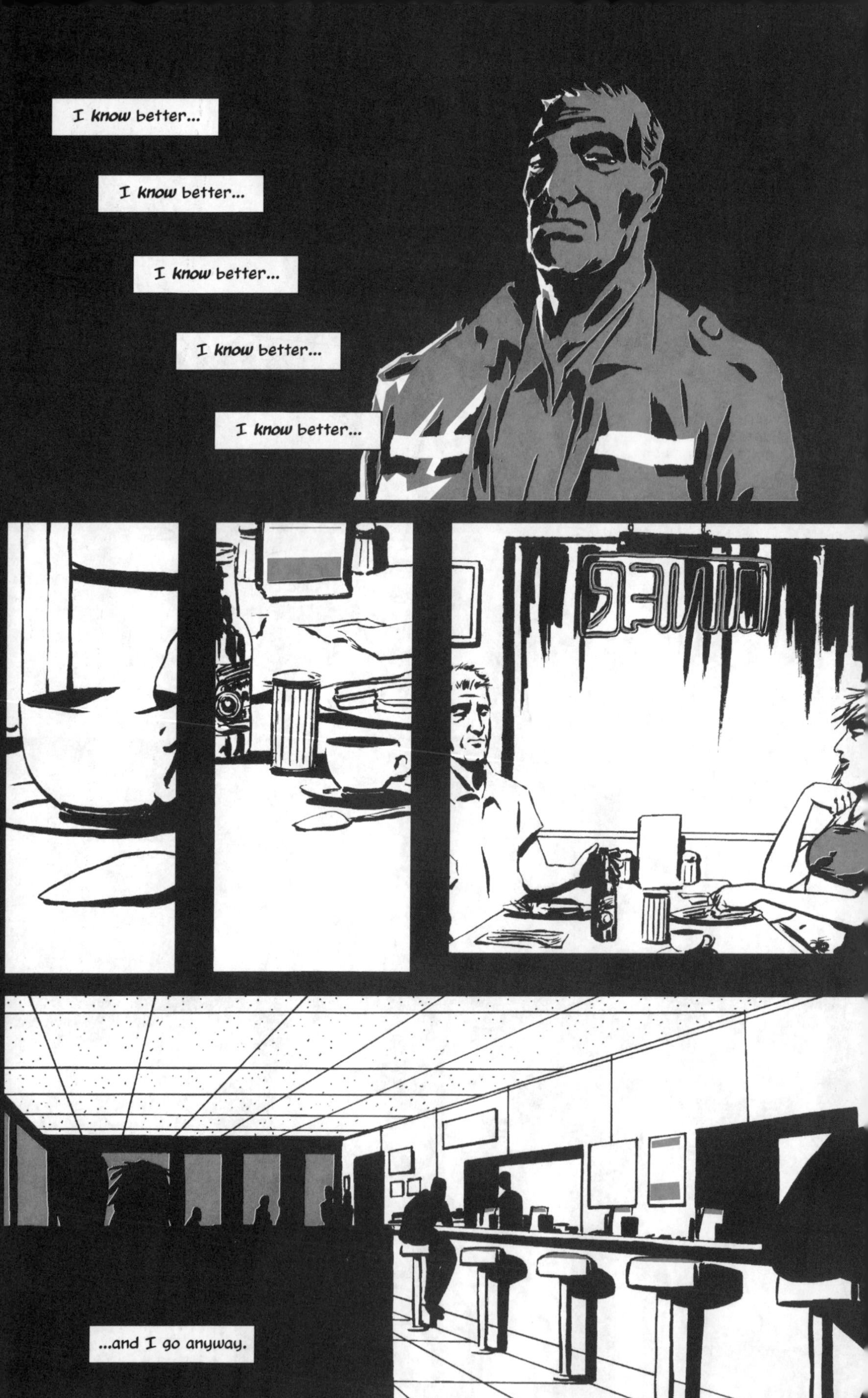
I know better...
I know better...
I know better...
I know better...
I know better...
...and I go anyway.

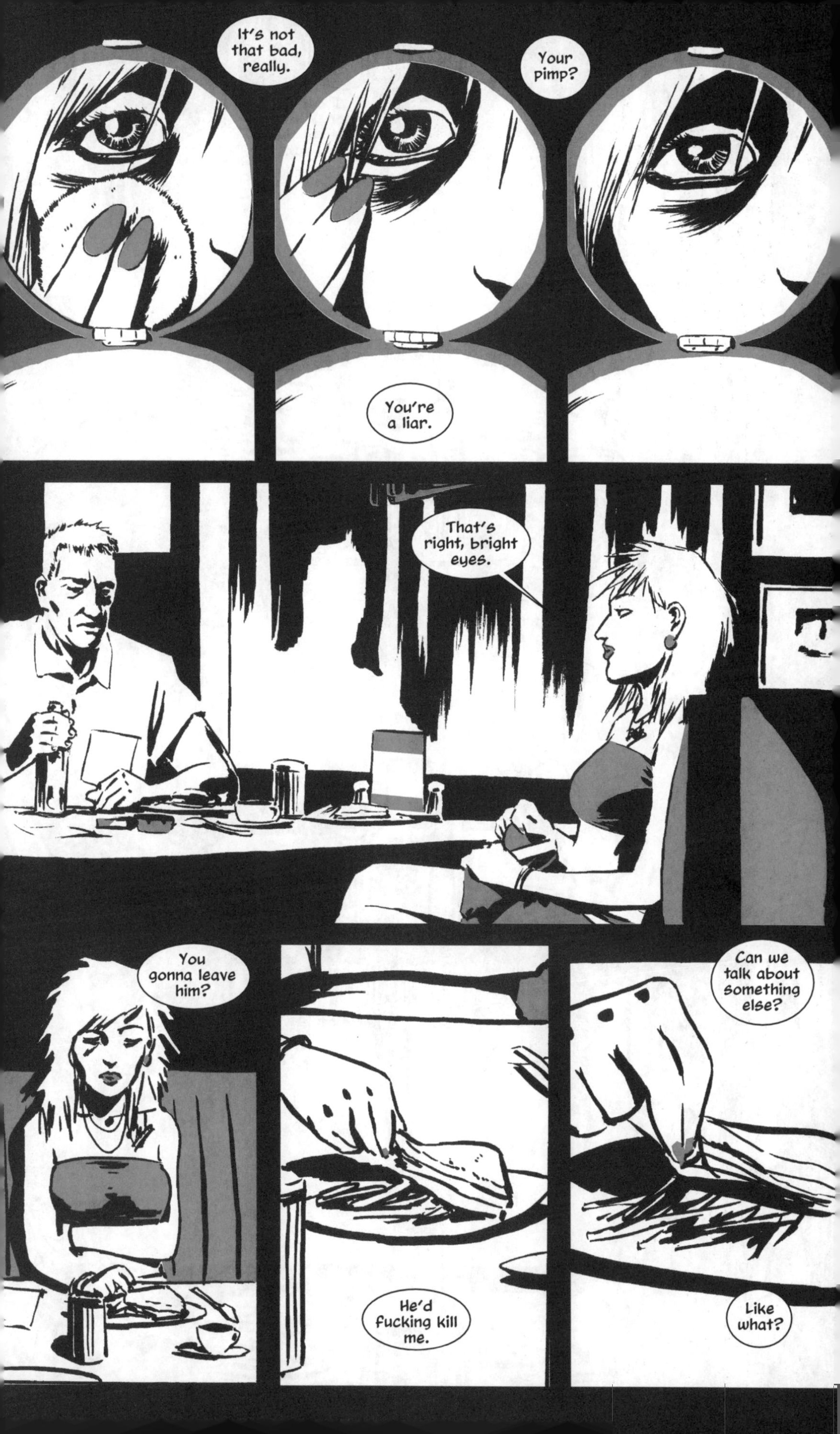
It's not that bad, really.
Your pimp?
You're a liar.
That's right, bright eyes.
You gonna leave him?
He'd fucking kill me.
Can we talk about something else?
Like what?

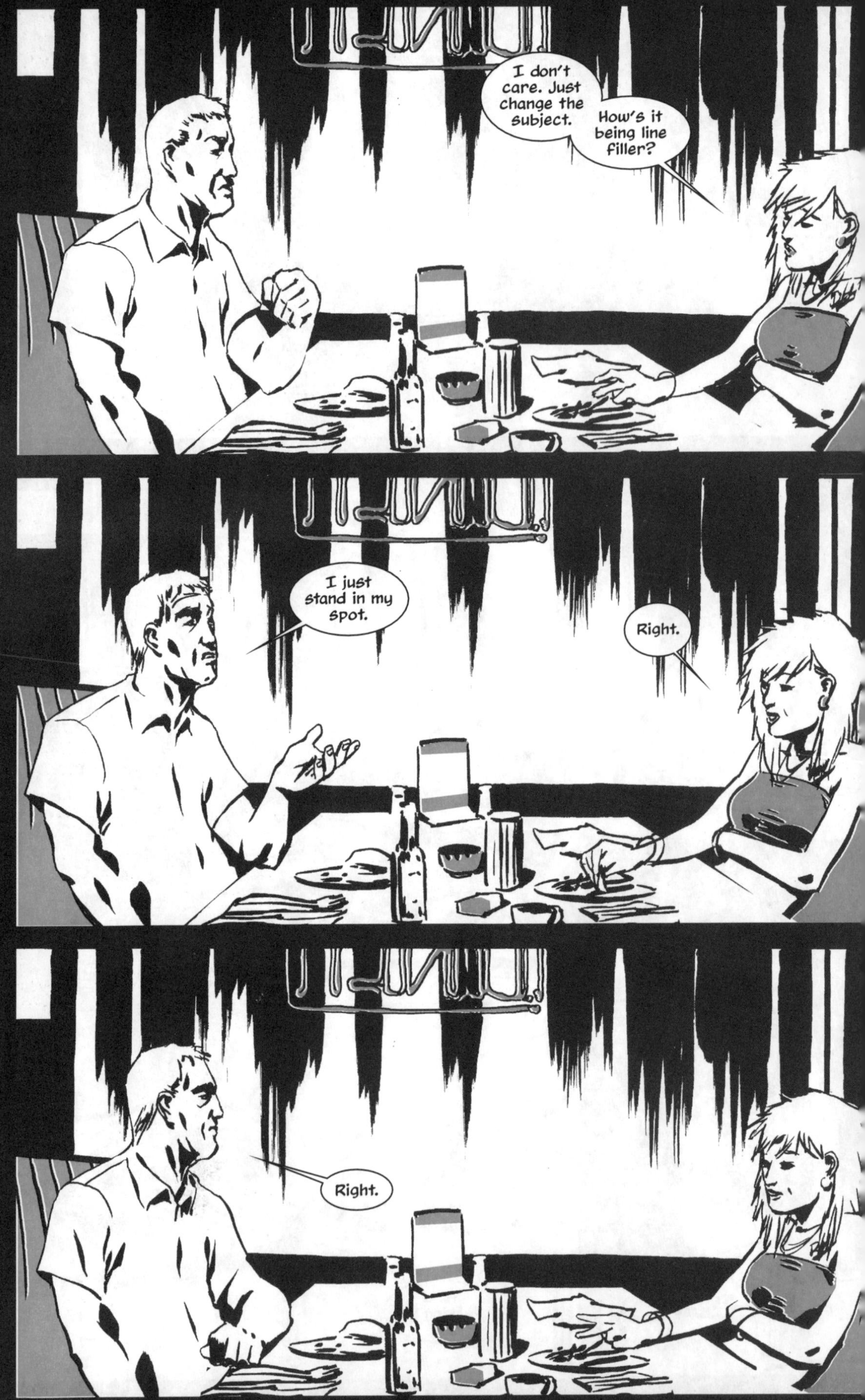
I don't care. Just change the subject.
How's it being line filler?
I just stand in my spot.
Right.
Right.

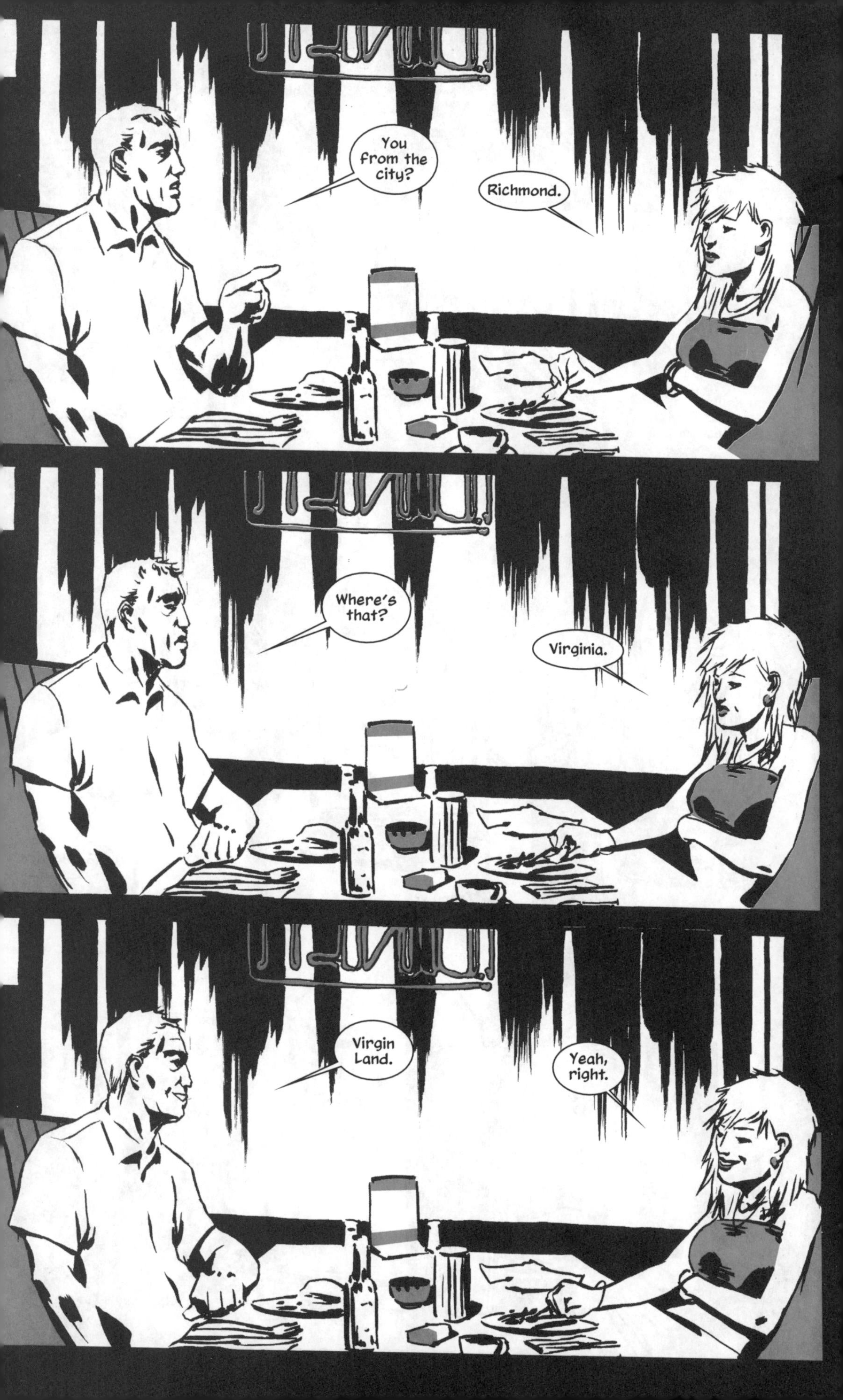
You from the city?
Richmond.
Where's that?
Virginia.
Virgin Land.
Yeah, right.

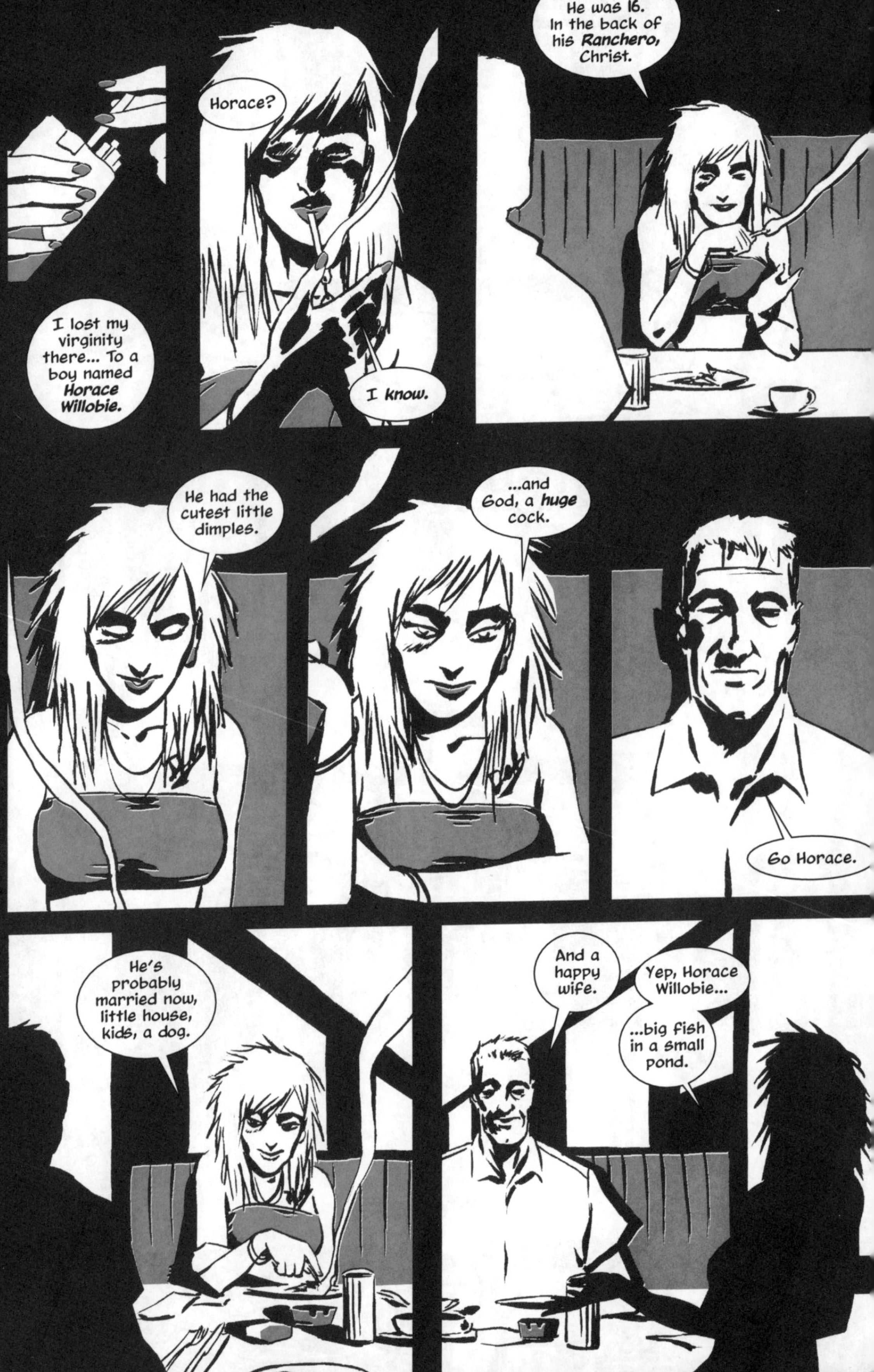
I lost my virginity there... To a boy named Horace Willobie.
Horace?
I know.
I was 14. He was 16. In the back of his Ranchero, Christ.
He had the cutest little dimples.
...and God, a huge cock.
Go Horace.
He's probably married now, little house, kids, a dog.
And a happy wife.
Yep, Horace Willobie...
...big fish in a small pond.

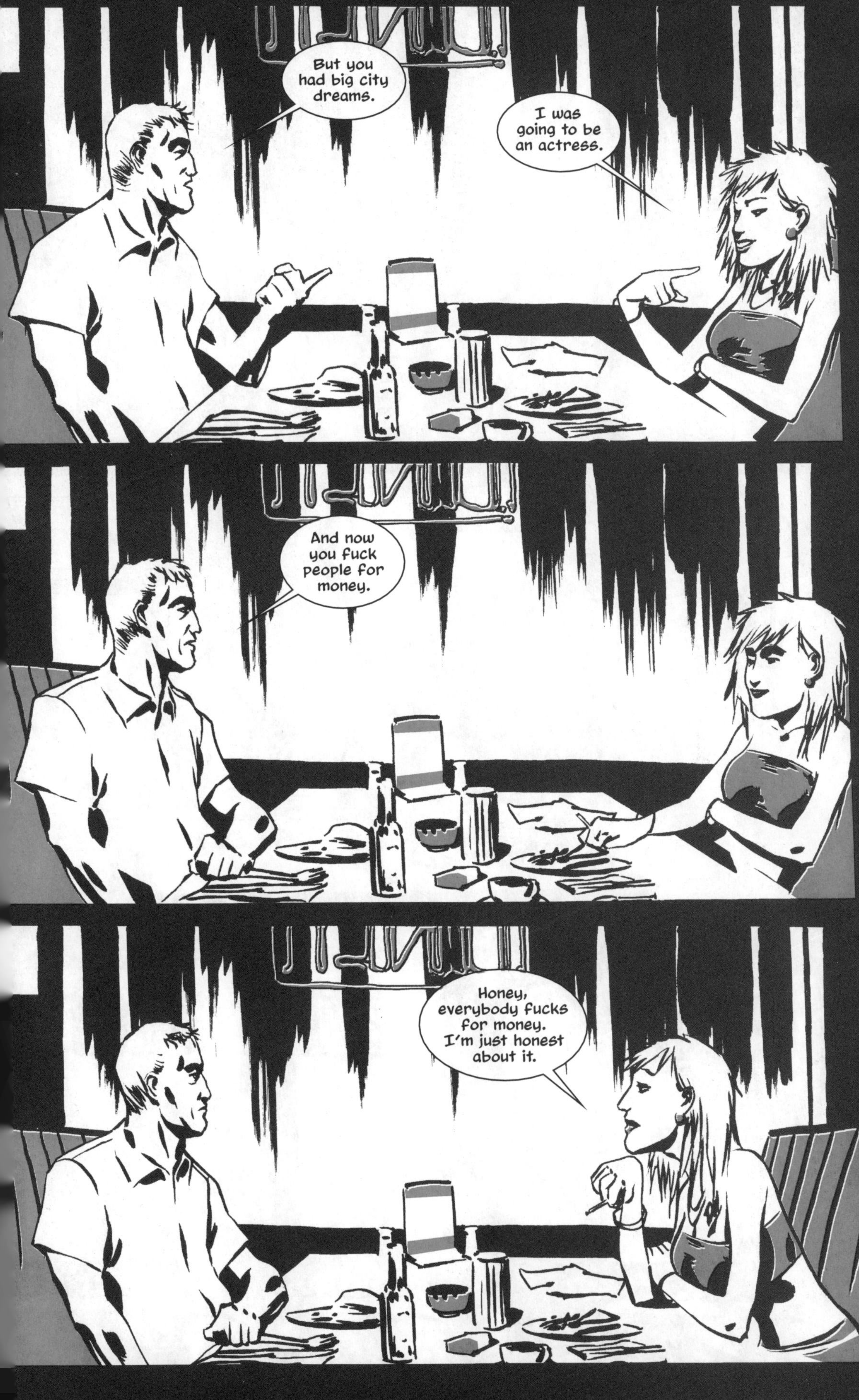
But you had big city dreams.
I was going to be an actress.
And now you fuck people for money.
Honey, everybody fucks for money. I'm just honest about it.

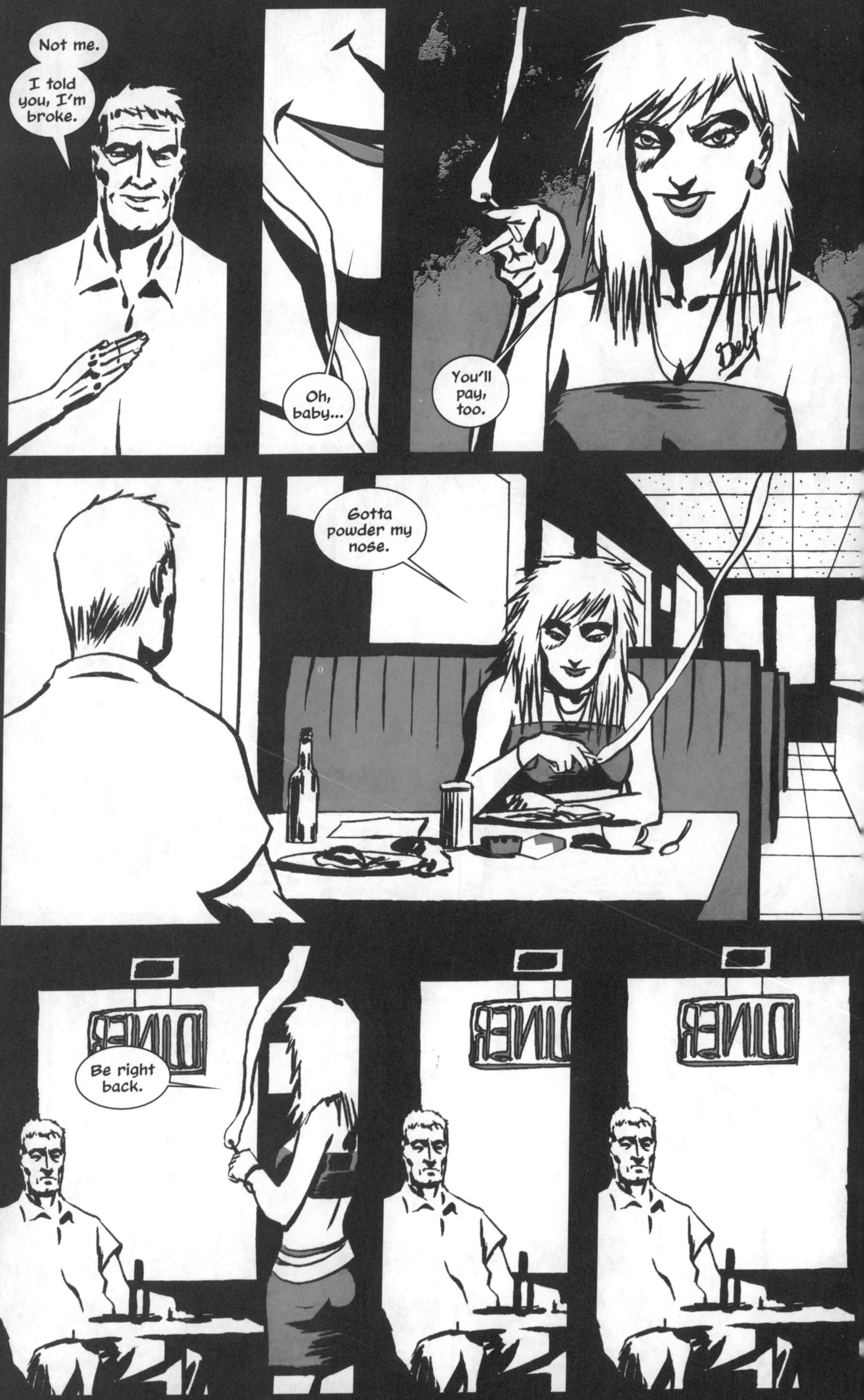
Not me.
I told you, I'm broke.
Oh, baby...
You'll pay, too.
Gotta powder my nose.
Be right back.

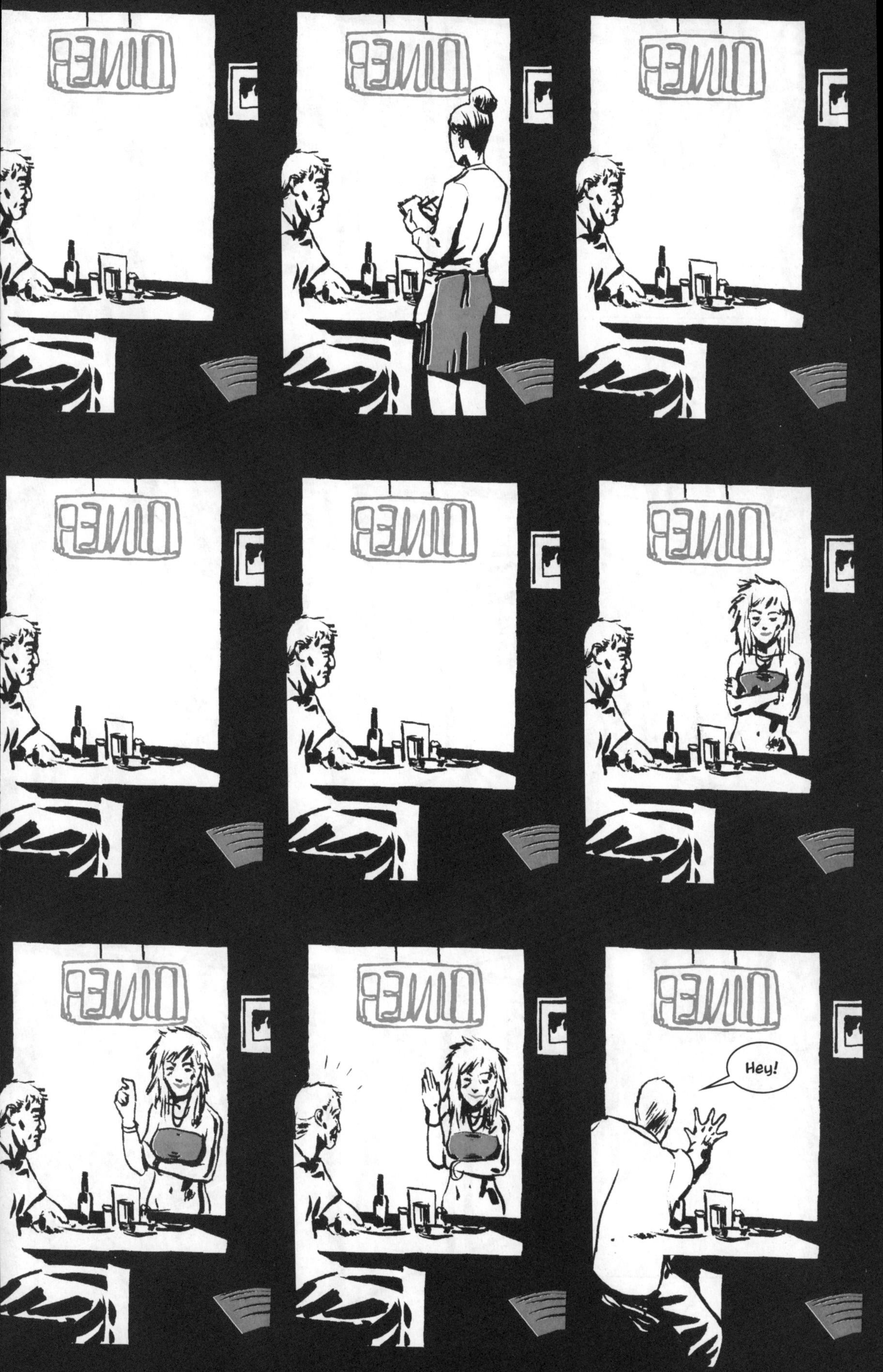
Hey!

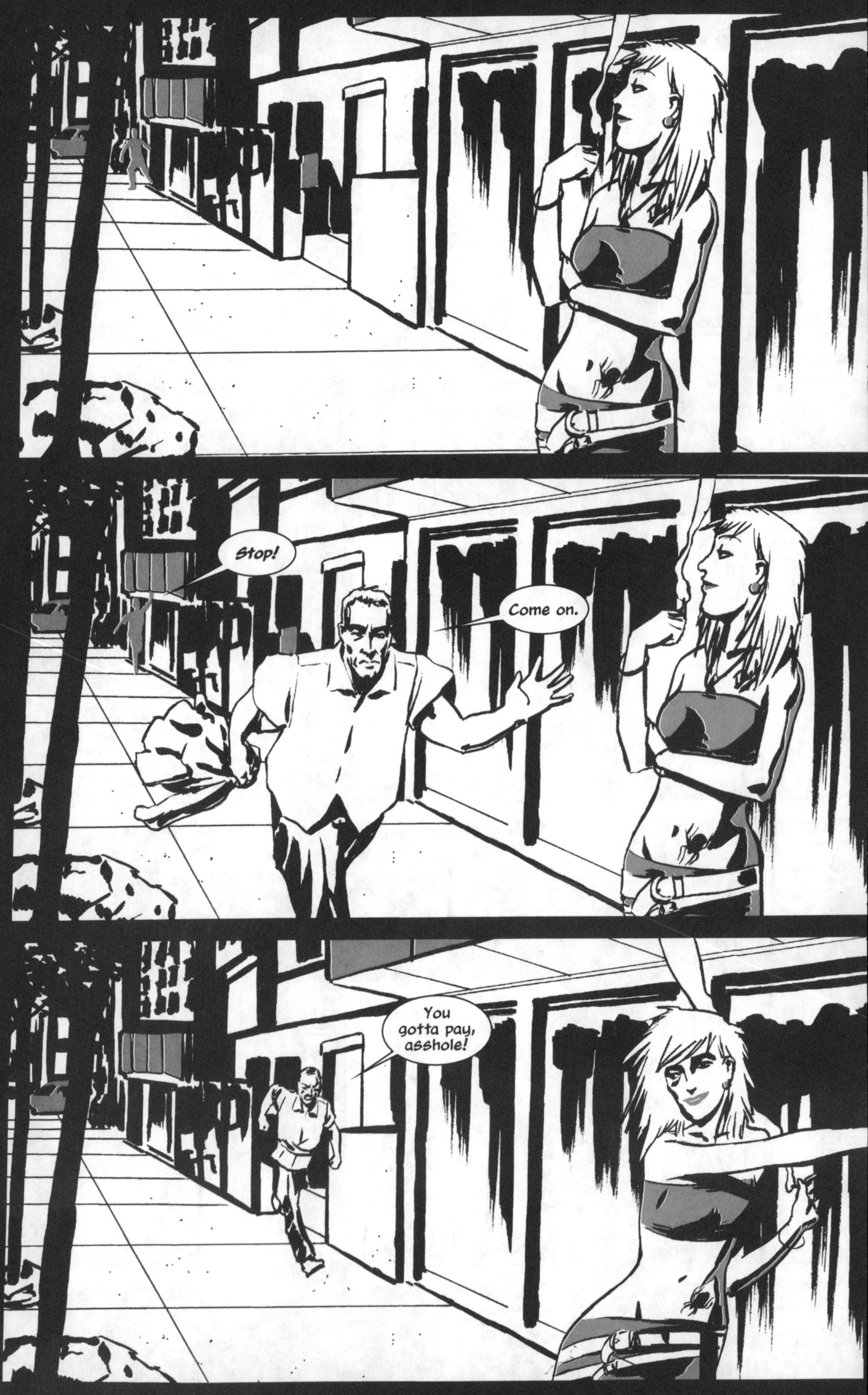
Stop!
Come on.
You gotta pay, asshole!

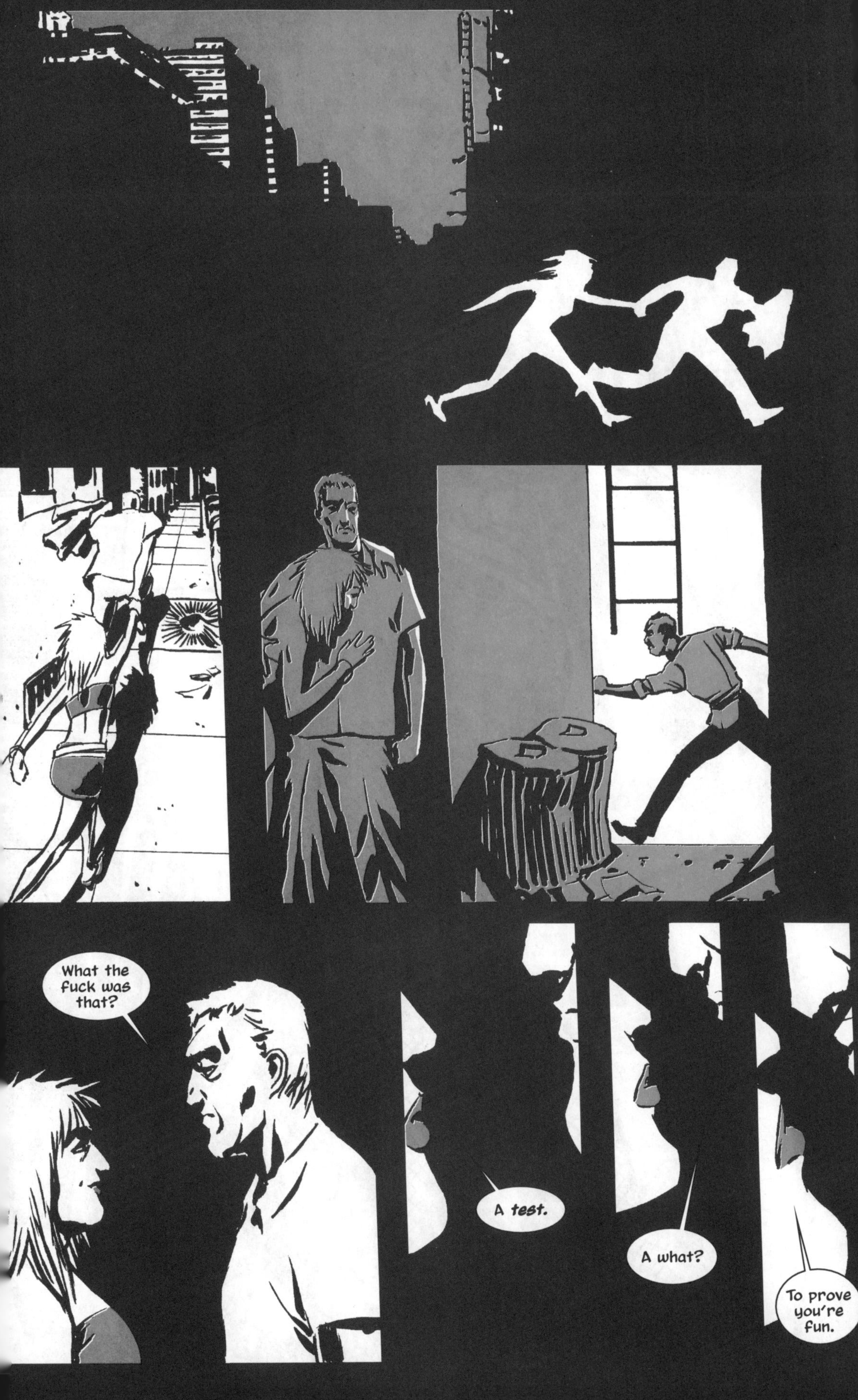
What the fuck was that?
A test.
A what?
To prove you're fun.

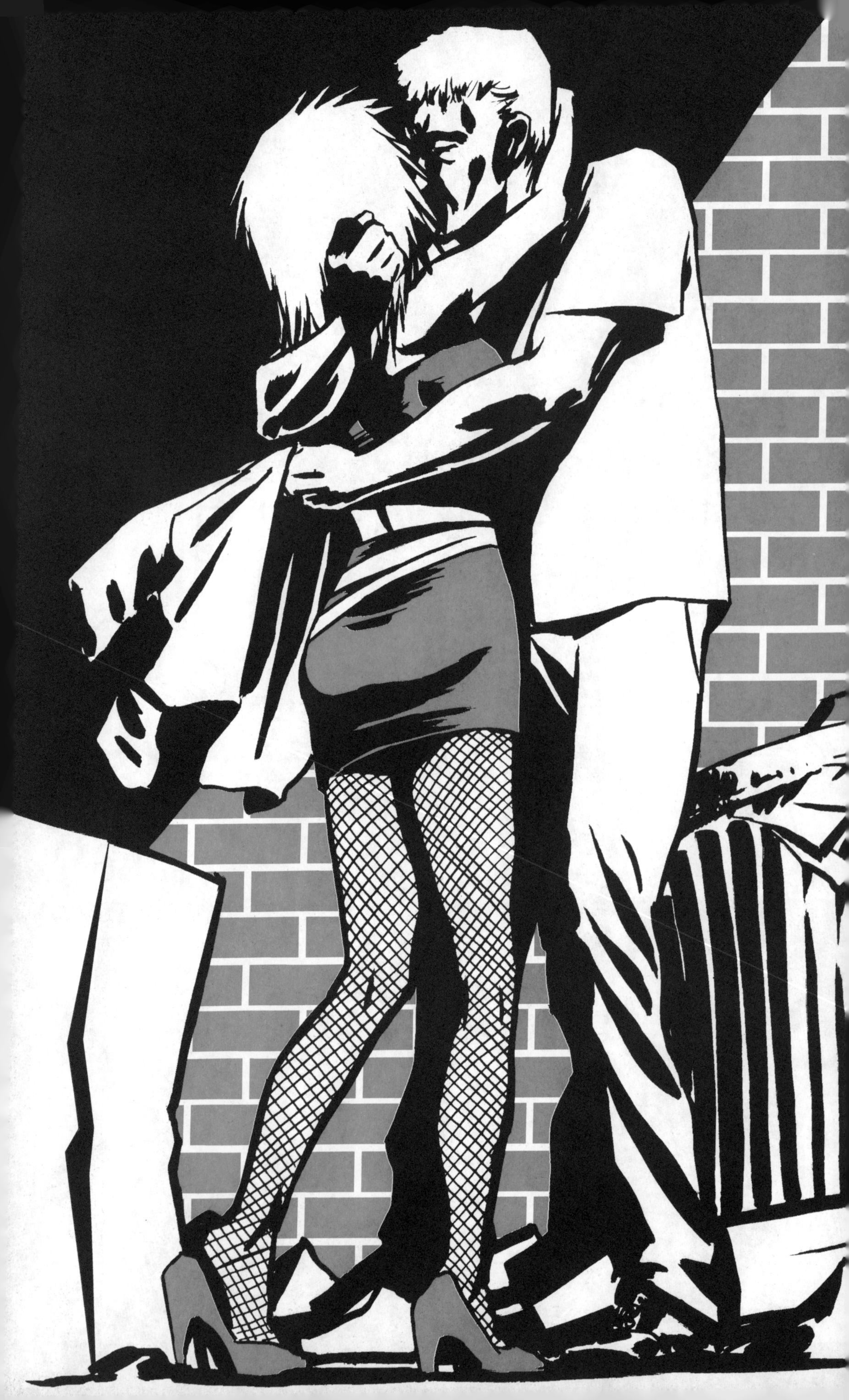

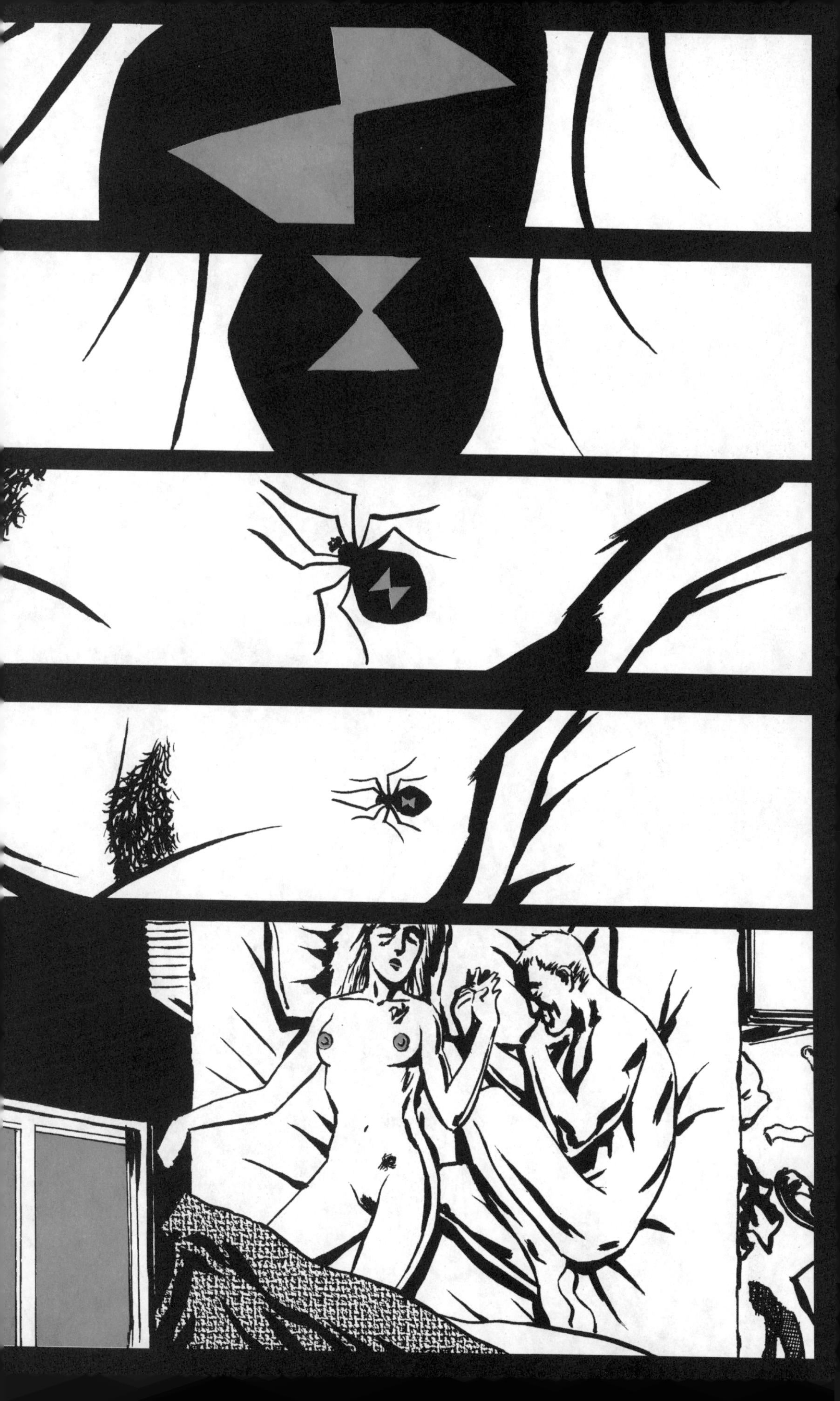

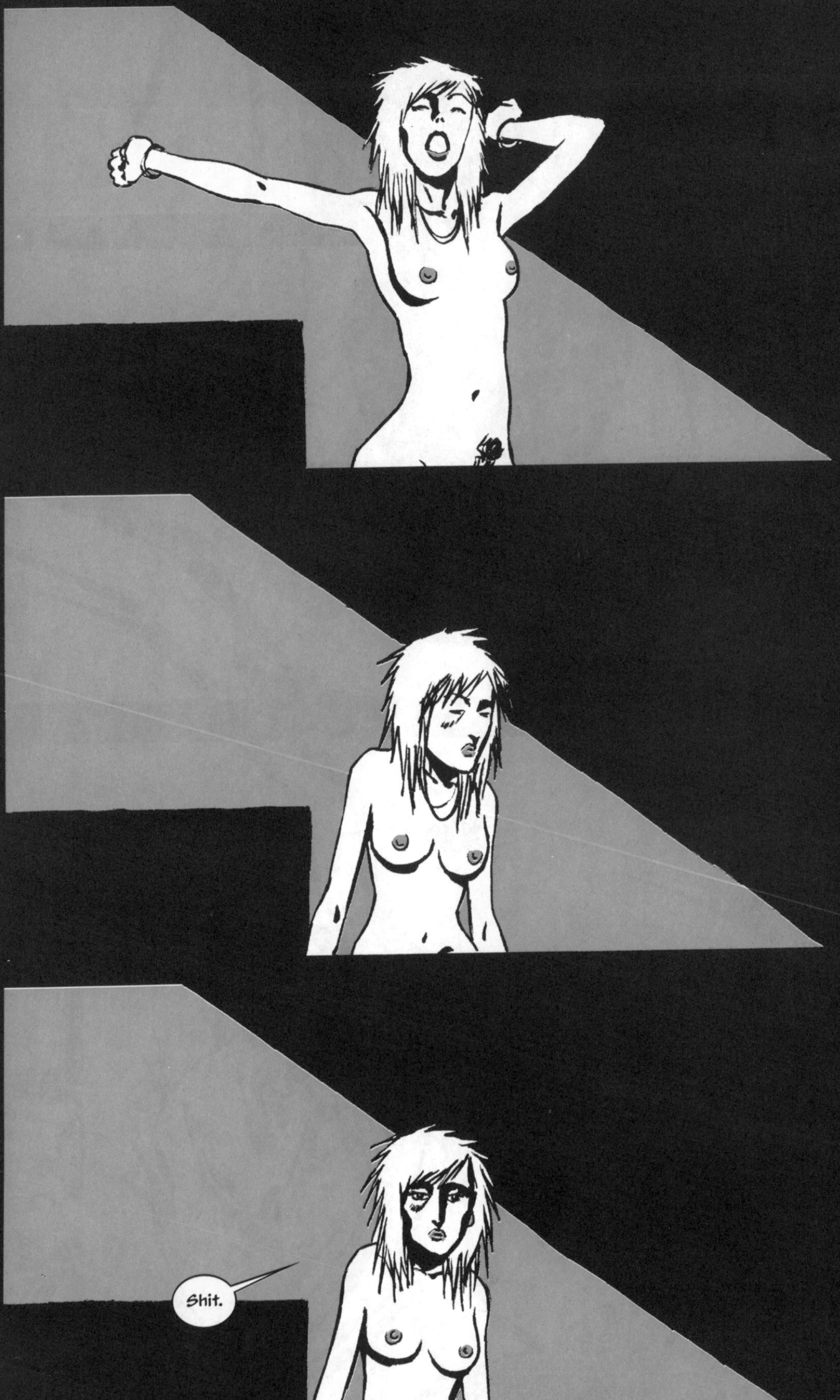
Shit.

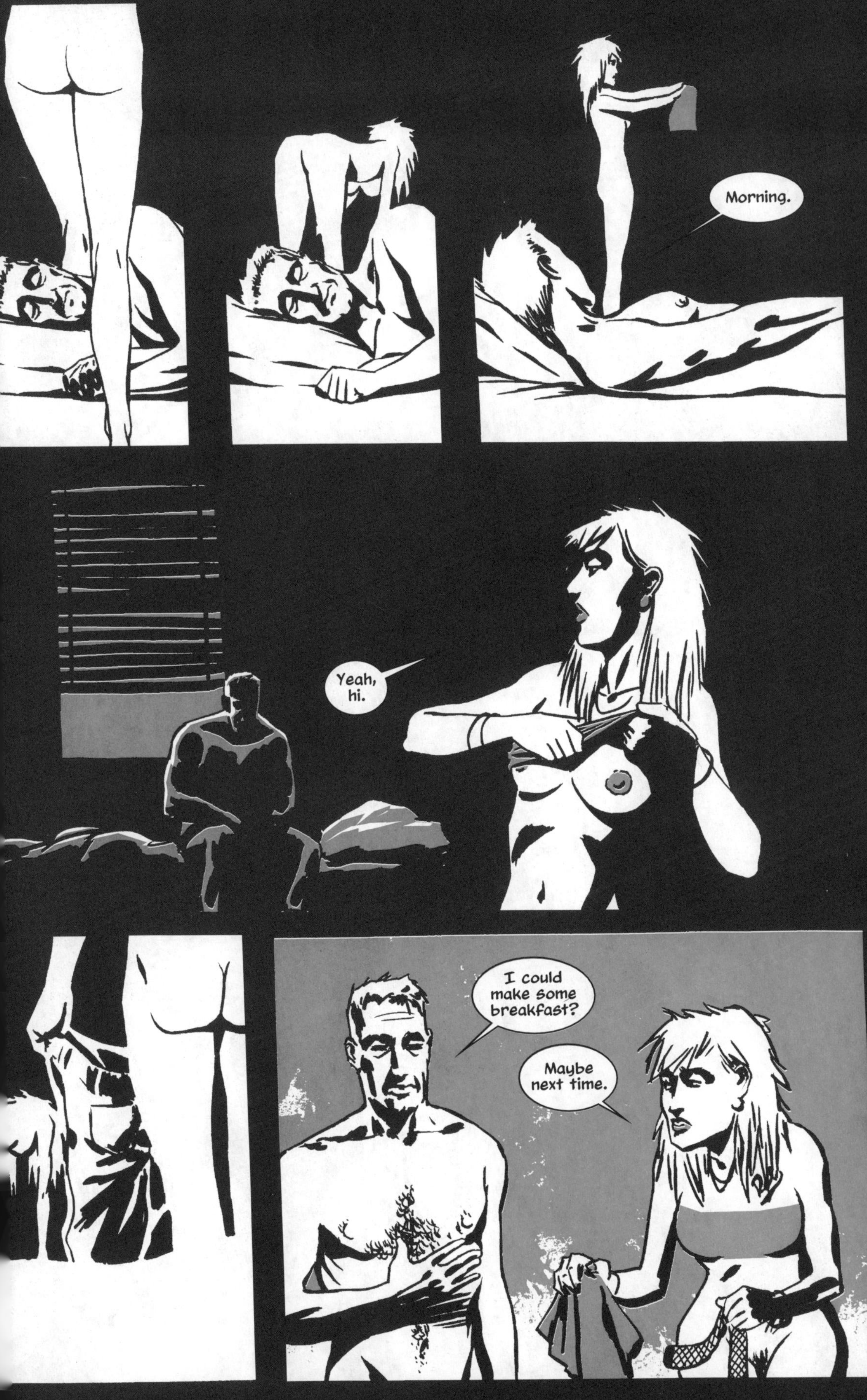
Morning.
Yeah, hi.
I could make some breakfast?
Maybe next time.

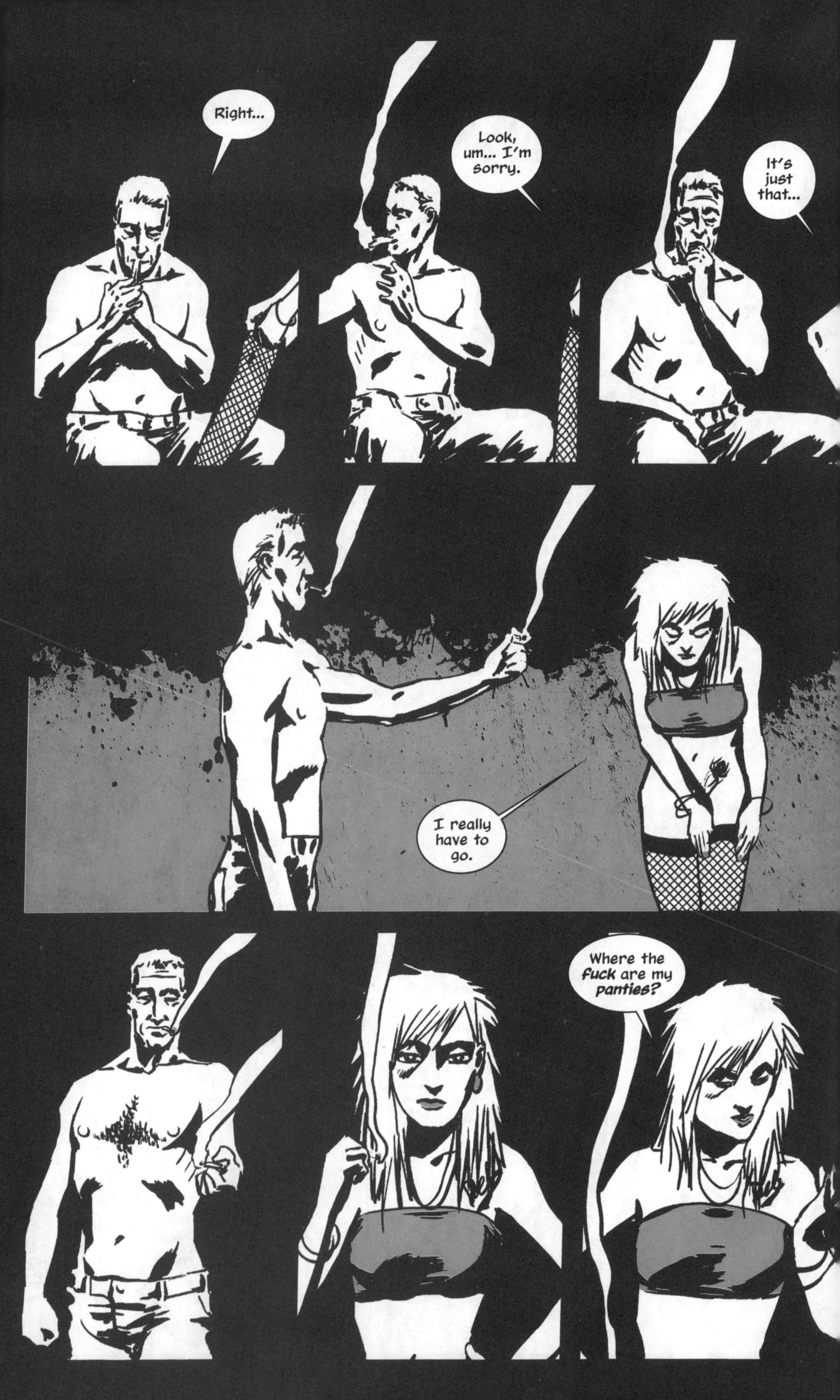
Right...
Look, um... I'm sorry.
It's just that...
I really have to go.
Where the fuck are my panties?

You have
o go back
to him?

If I get
back before
he's up he
might be
cool.

Will
he hurt
you?

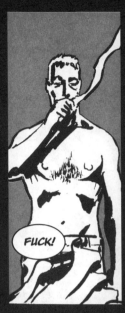

FUCK!

OK, I can't
find my panties,
so Merry
Christmas. Don't
do anything
weird with
'em.

You're
not a *sniffer*,
are you?

Will he
hurt you?

Look, I
don't know.
OK....

I didn't
exactly make
my quota.

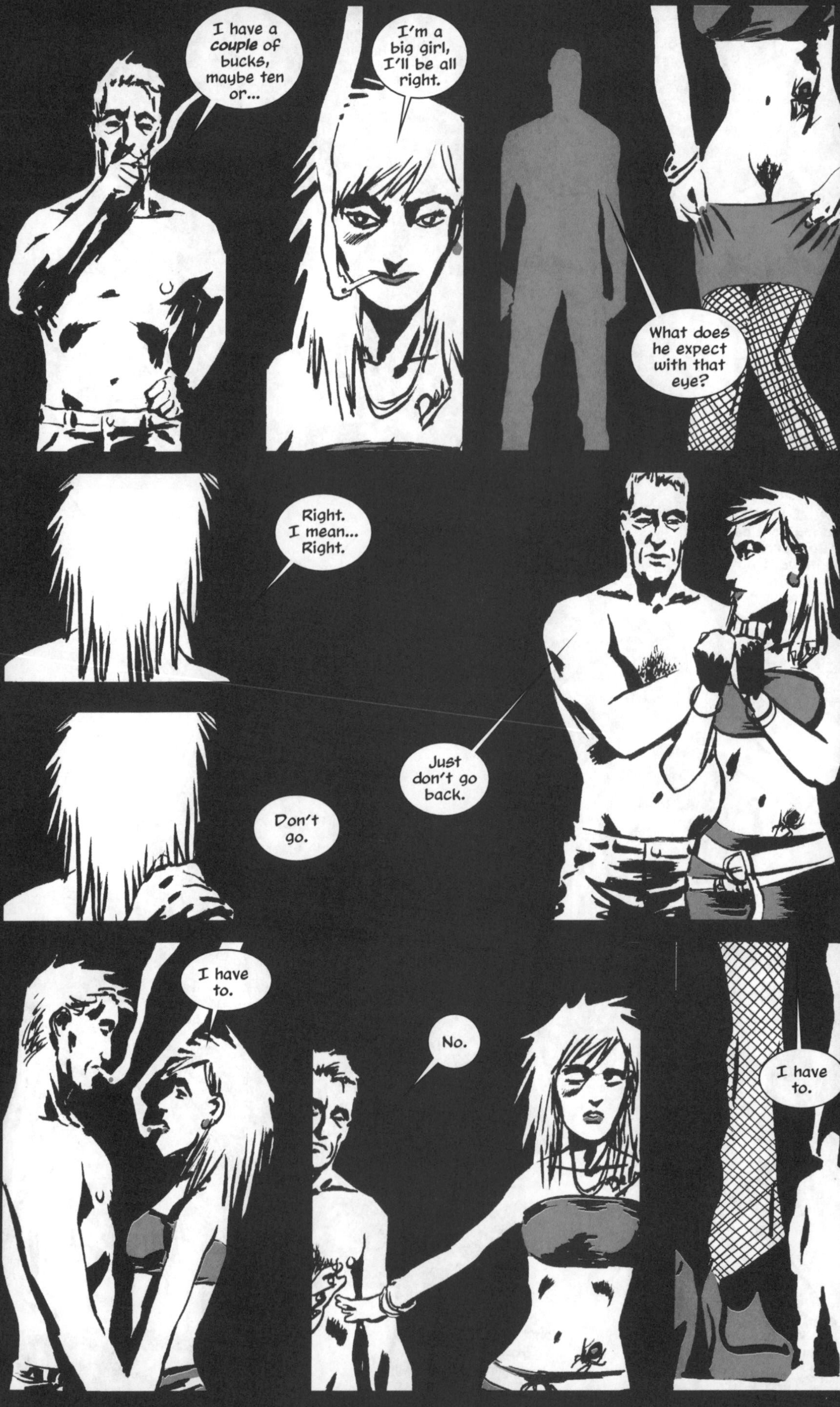
I have a *couple* of bucks, maybe ten or...
I'm a big girl, I'll be all right.
What does he expect with that eye?
Right. I mean... Right.
Just don't go back.
Don't go.
I have to.
No.
I have to.

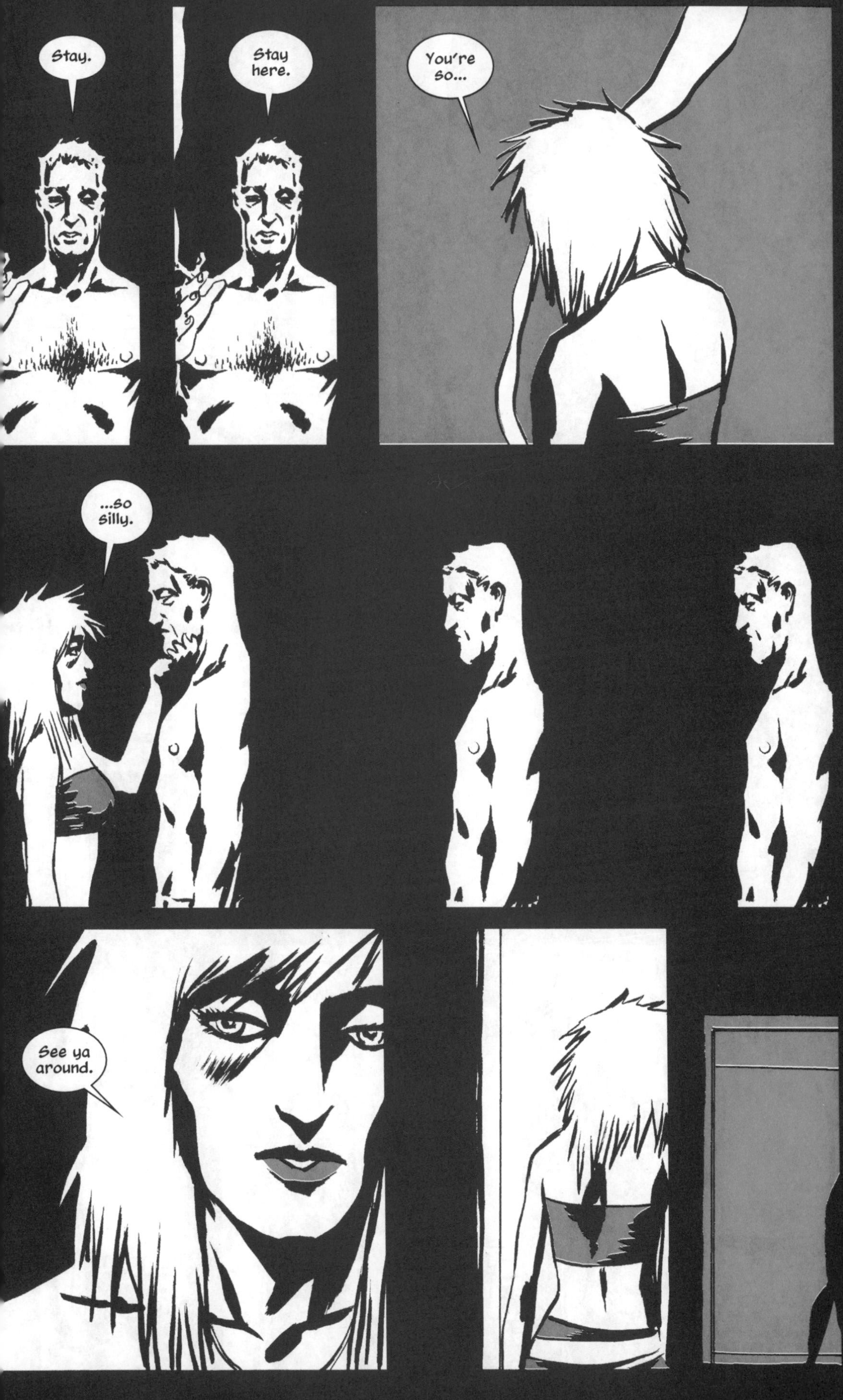
Stay.
Stay here.
You're so...
...so silly.
See ya around.

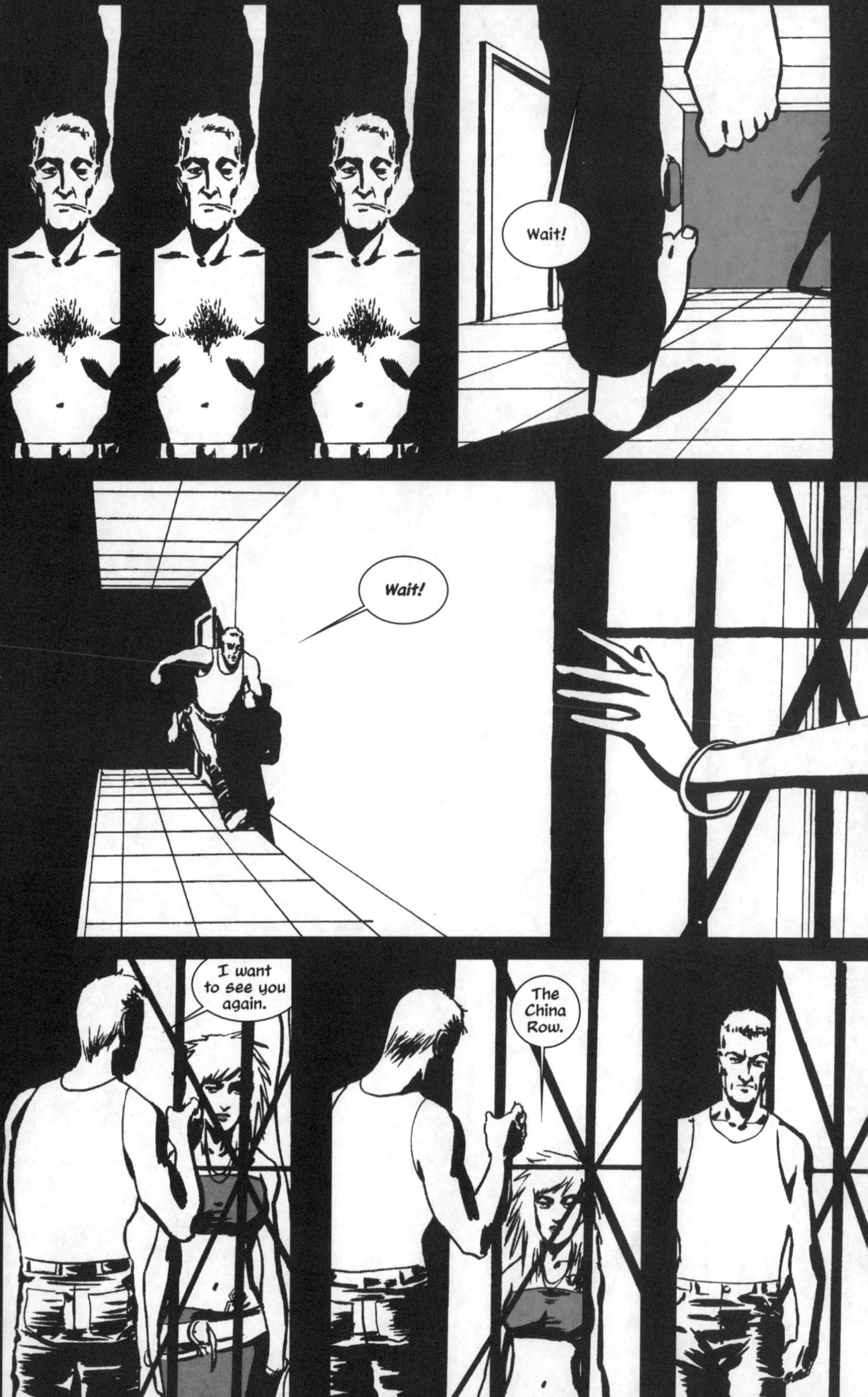
Wait!
Wait!
I want to see you again.
The China Row.

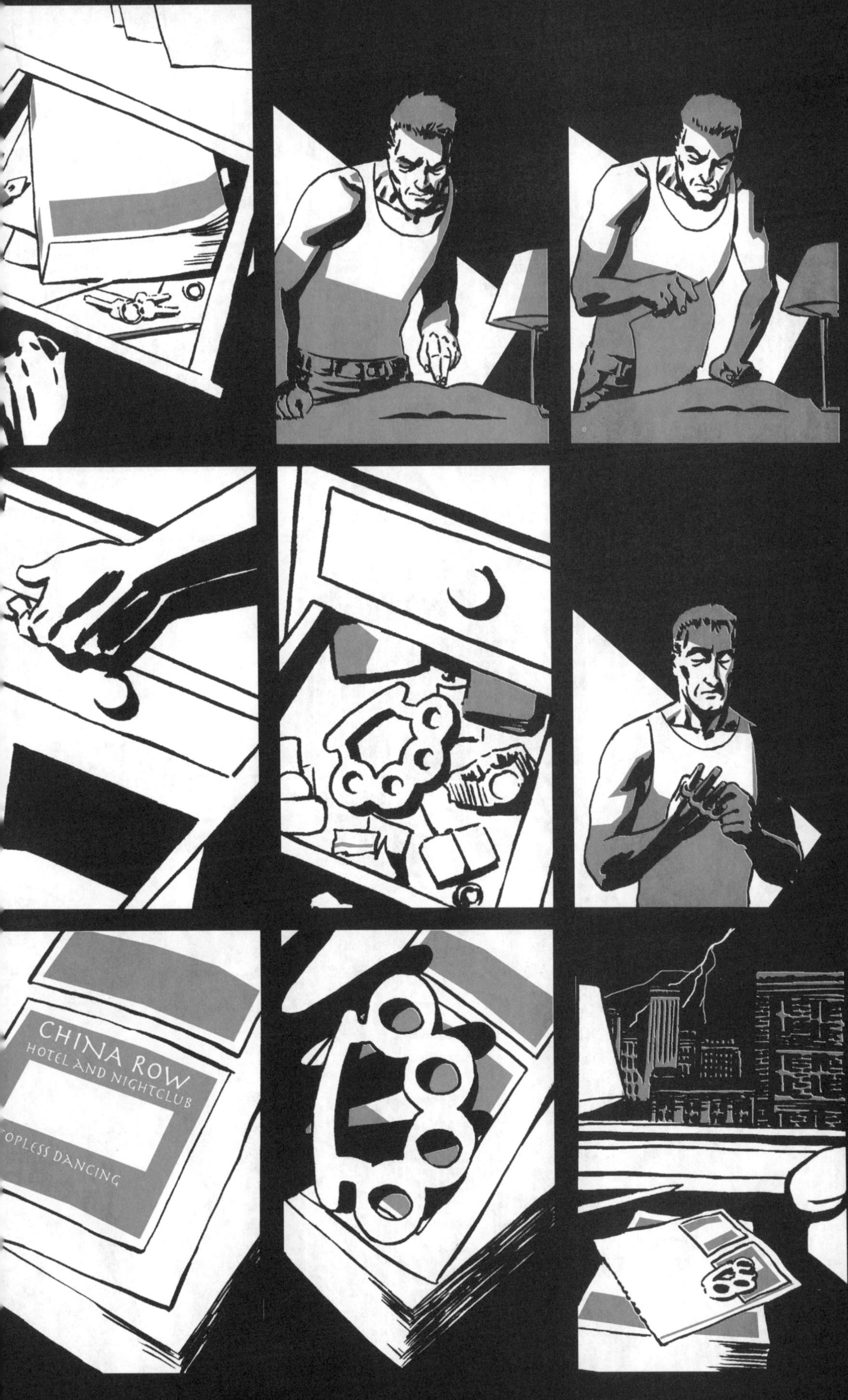
CHINA ROW
HOTEL AND NIGHTCLUB
OPLESS DANCING

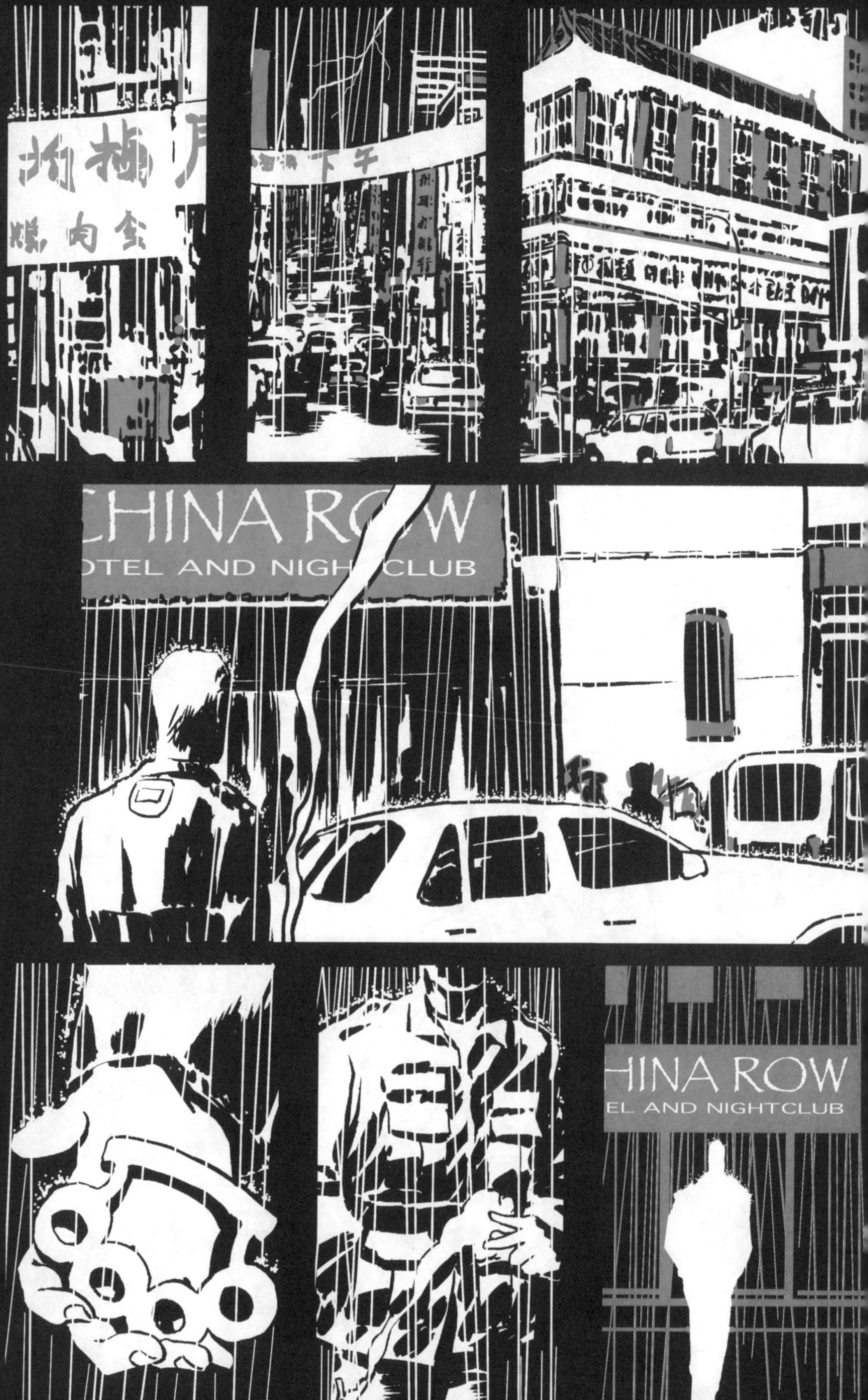
下午
CHINA ROW
OTEL AND NIGH CLUB
HINA ROW
EL AND NIGHTCLUB

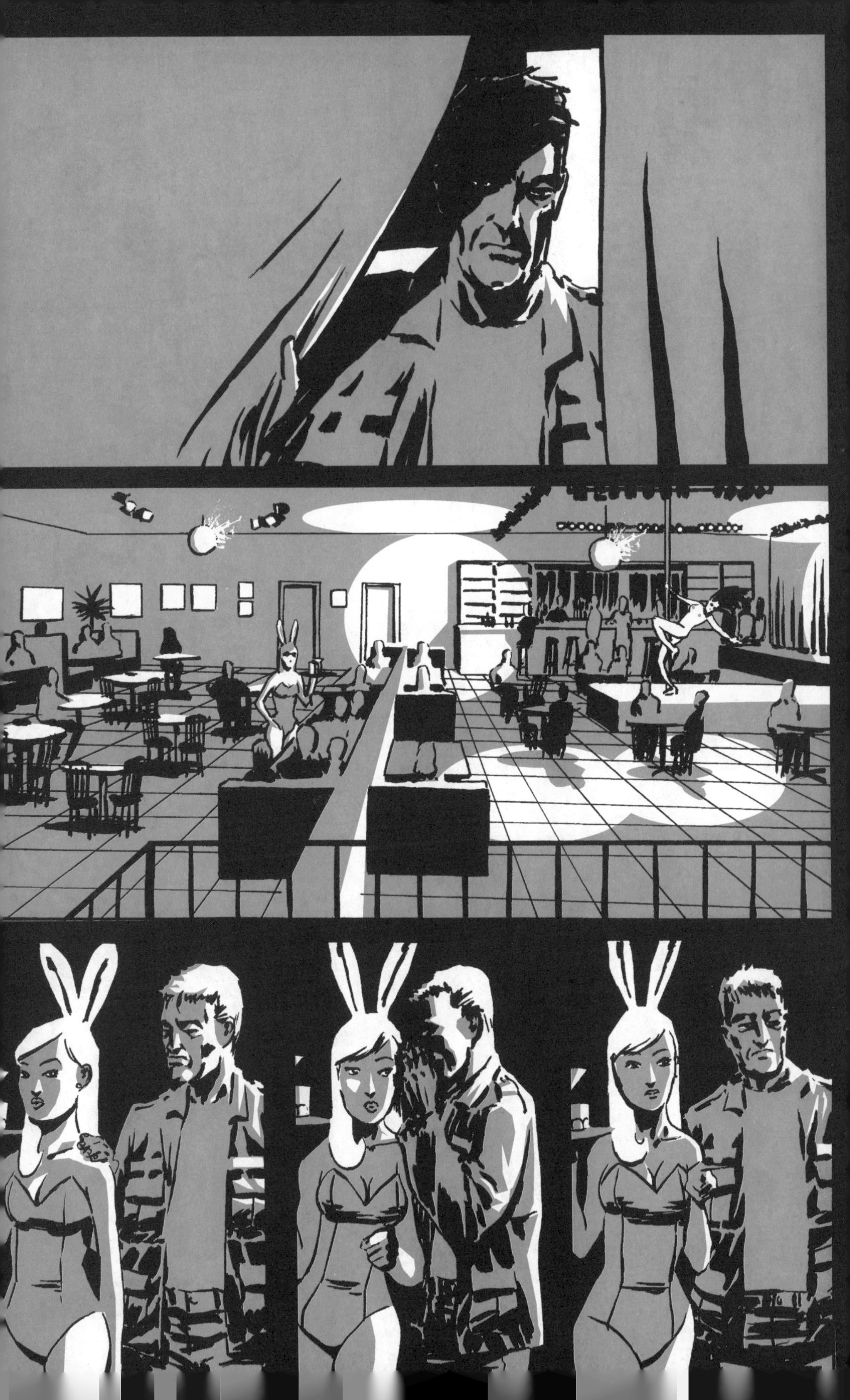

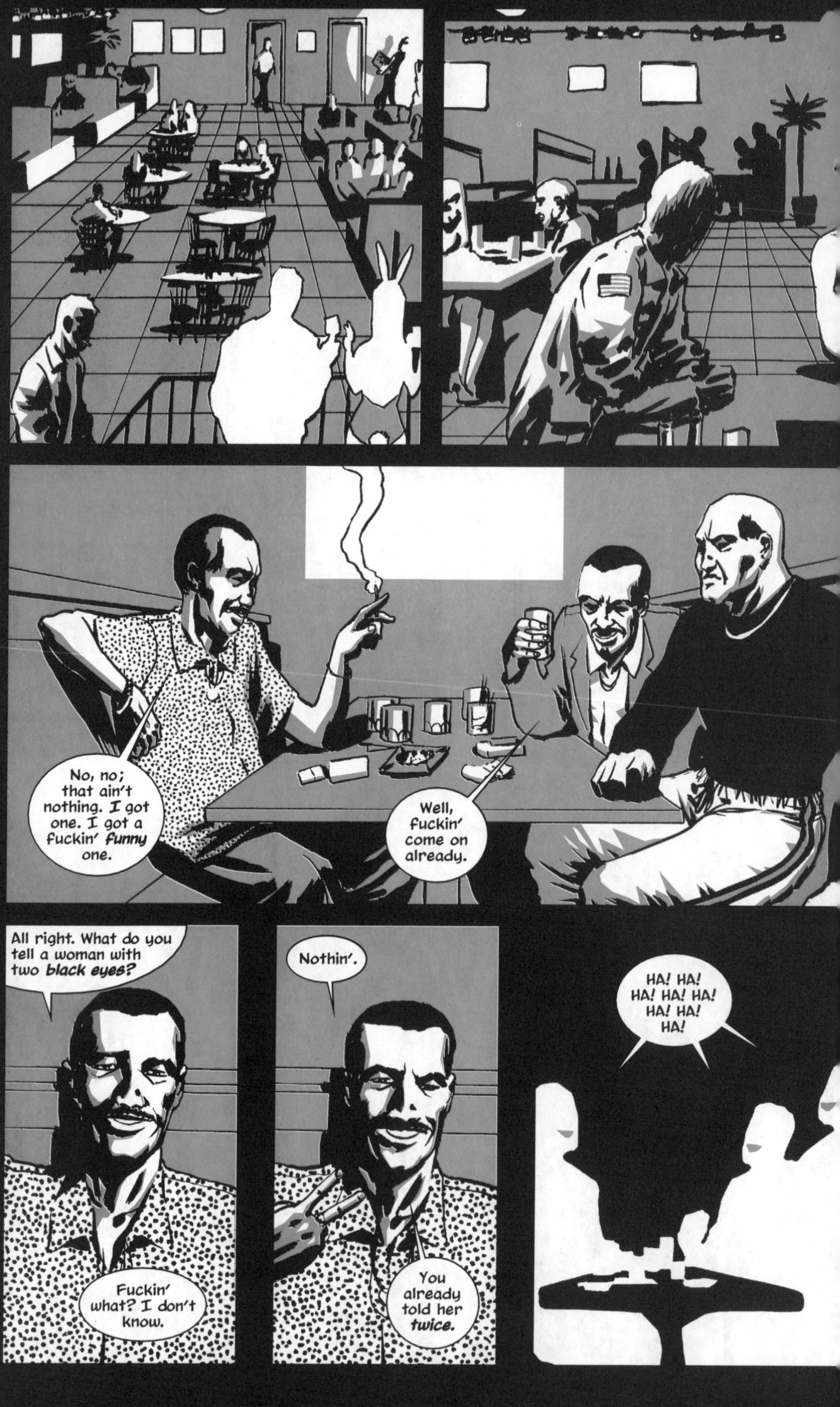

No, no; that ain't nothing. I got one. I got a fuckin' *funny* one.
Well, fuckin' come on already.
All right. What do you tell a woman with two ***black eyes?***
Fuckin' what? I don't know.
Nothin'.
You already told her ***twice.***
HA! HA! HA! HA! HA! HA! HA! HA!

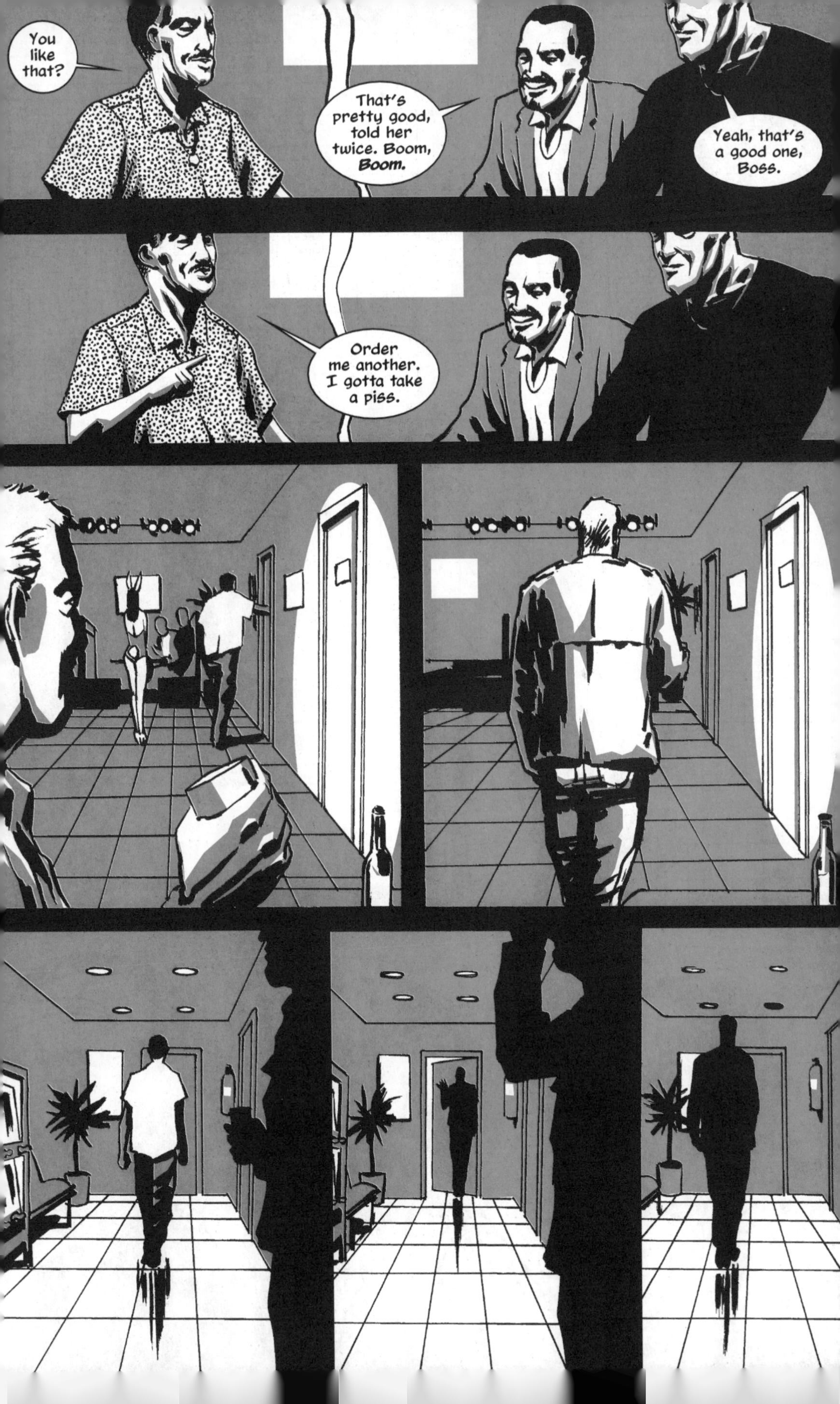
You like that?
That's pretty good, told her twice. Boom, **Boom.**
Yeah, that's a good one, Boss.
Order me another. I gotta take a piss.

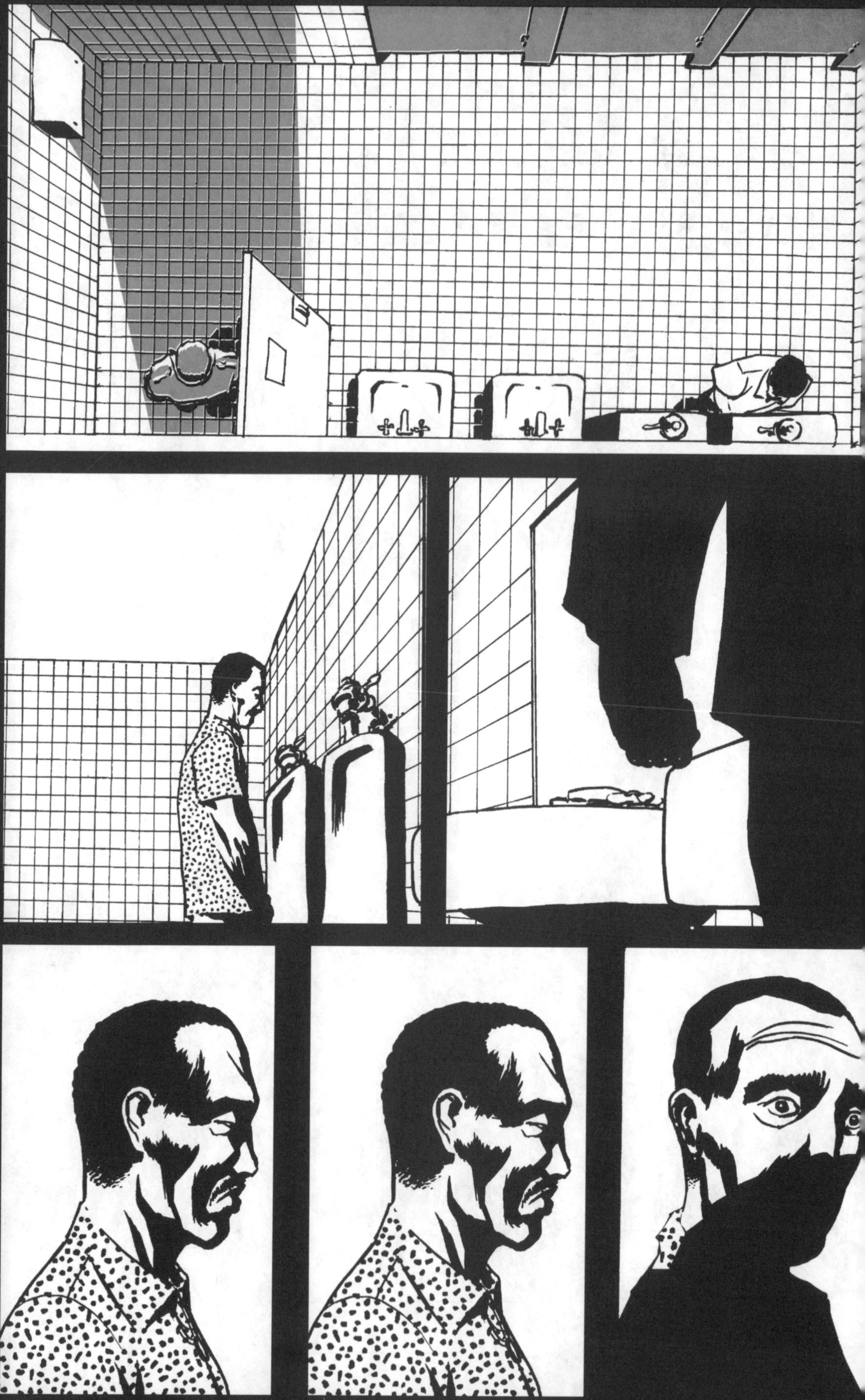

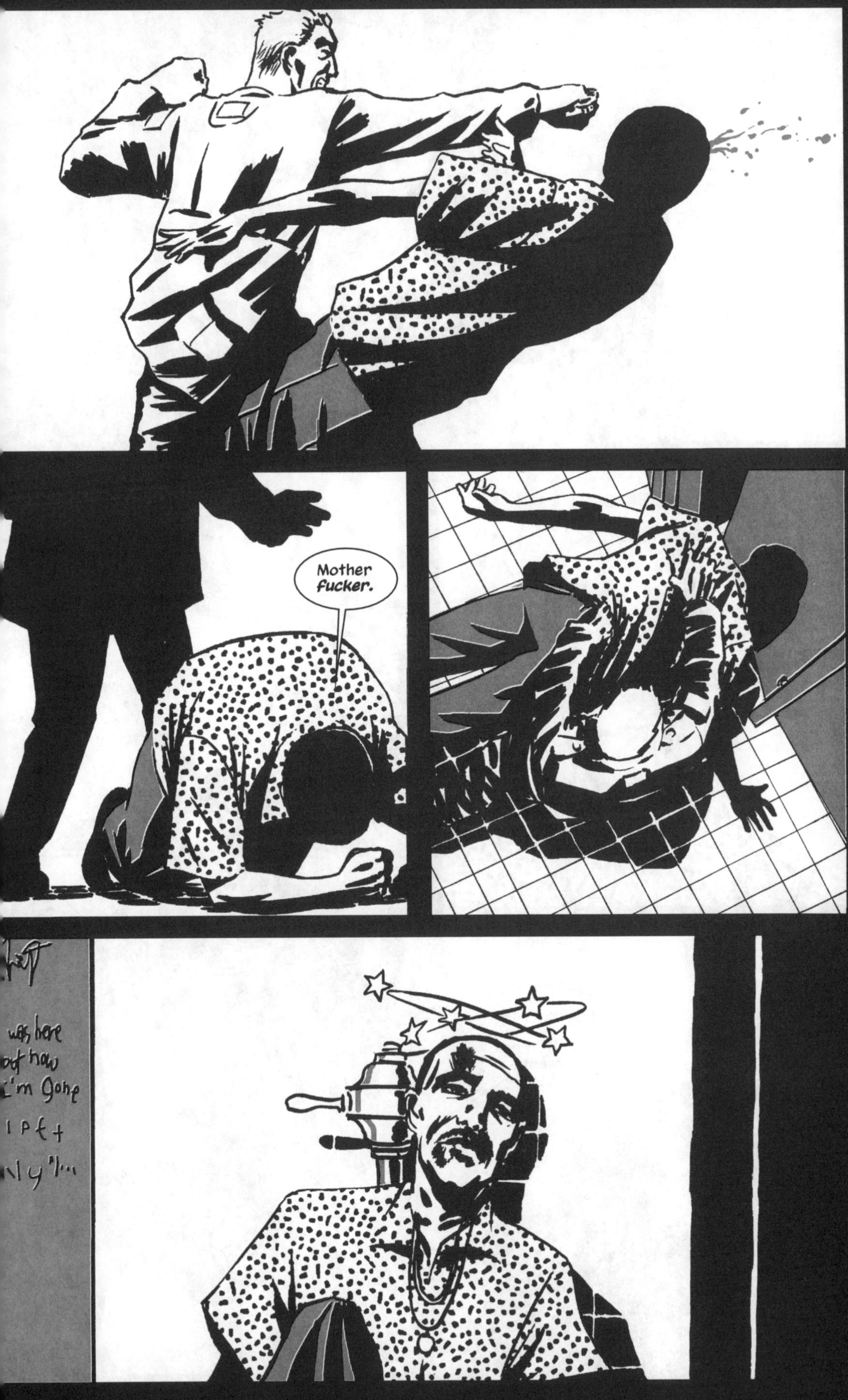
Mother fucker.

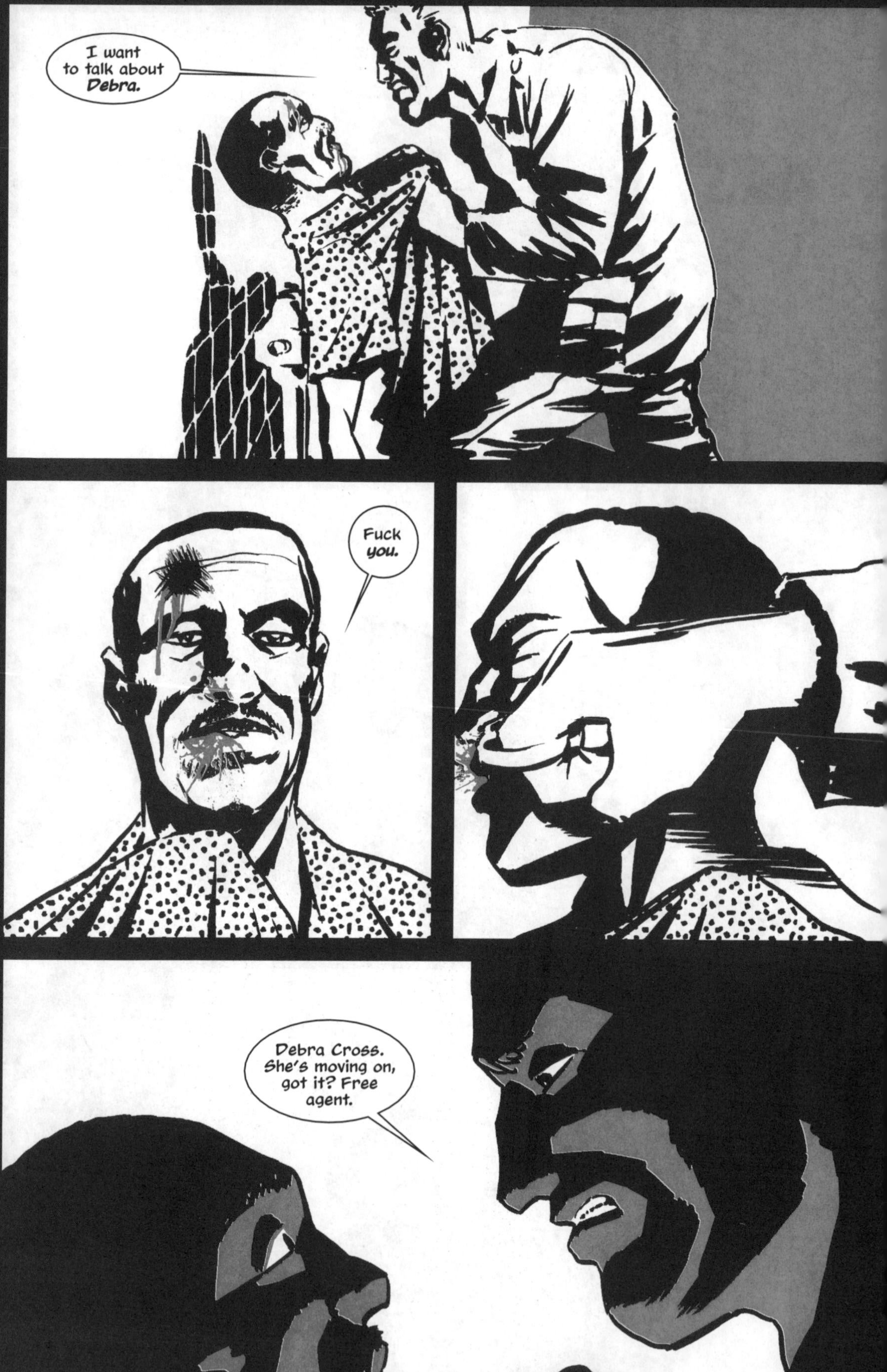
I want to talk about *Debra.*
Fuck *you.*
Debra Cross. She's moving on, got it? Free agent.

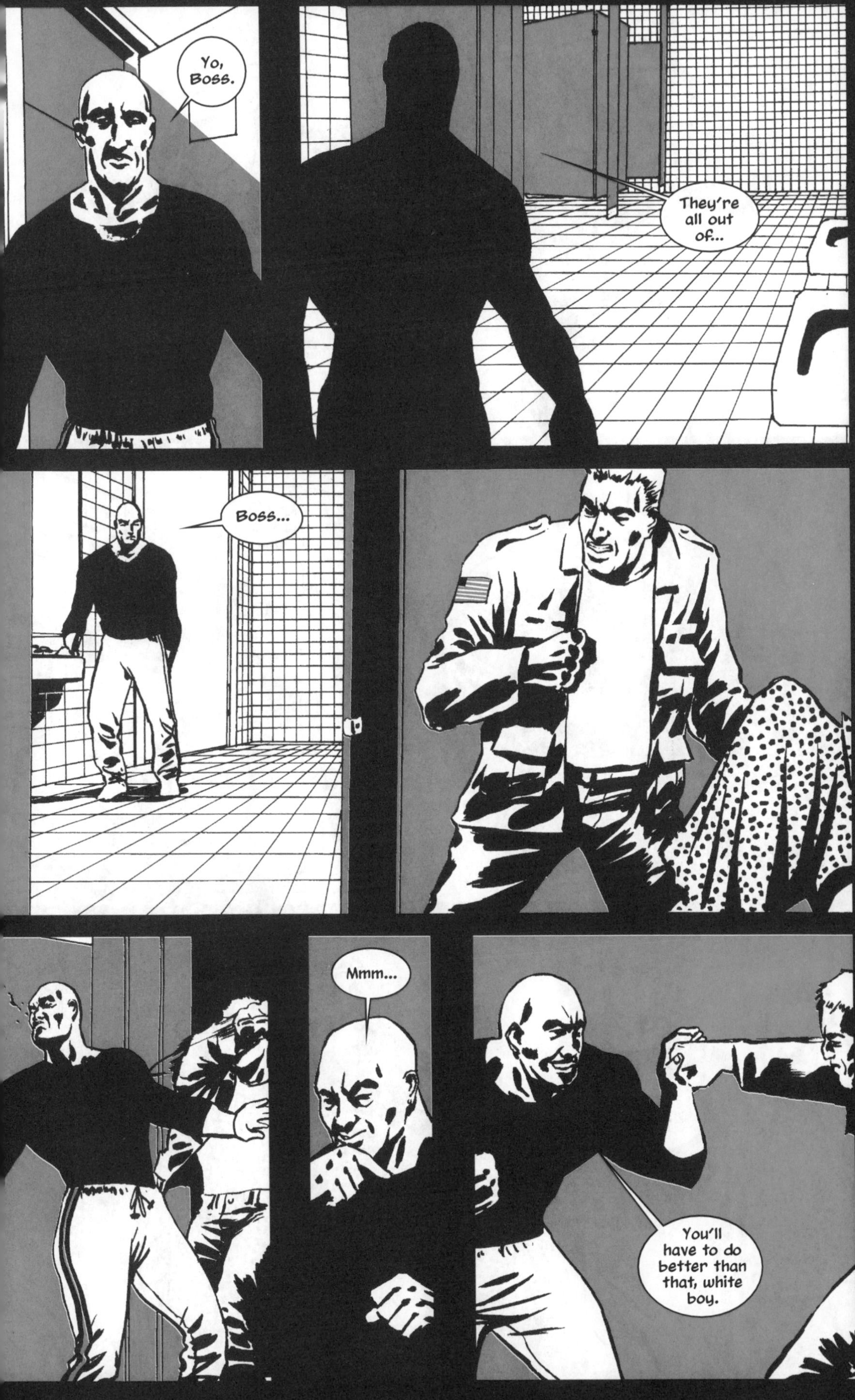
Yo, Boss.
They're all out of...
Boss...
Mmm...
You'll have to do better than that, white boy.

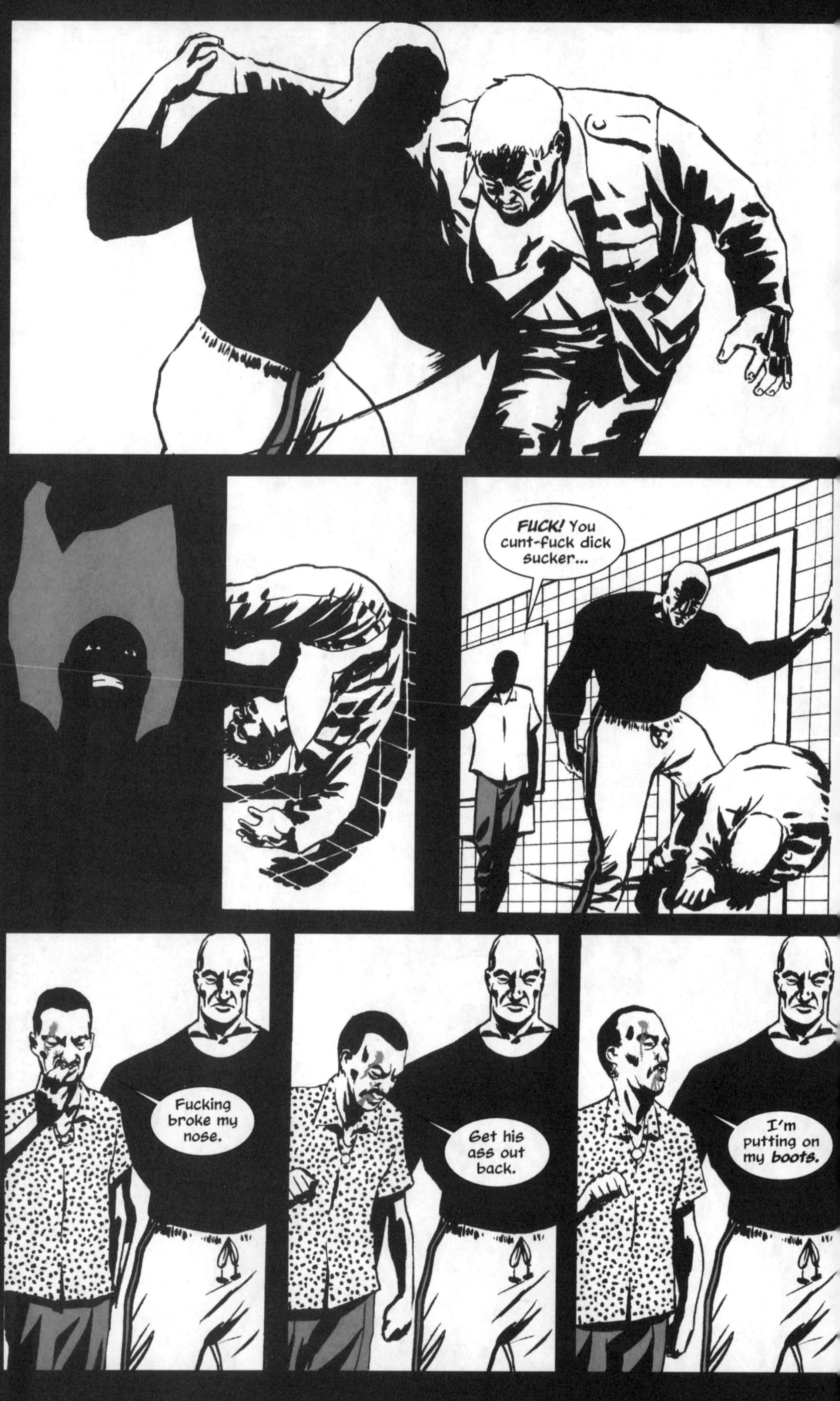
FUCK! You cunt-fuck dick sucker...
Fucking broke my nose.
Get his ass out back.
I'm putting on my boots.

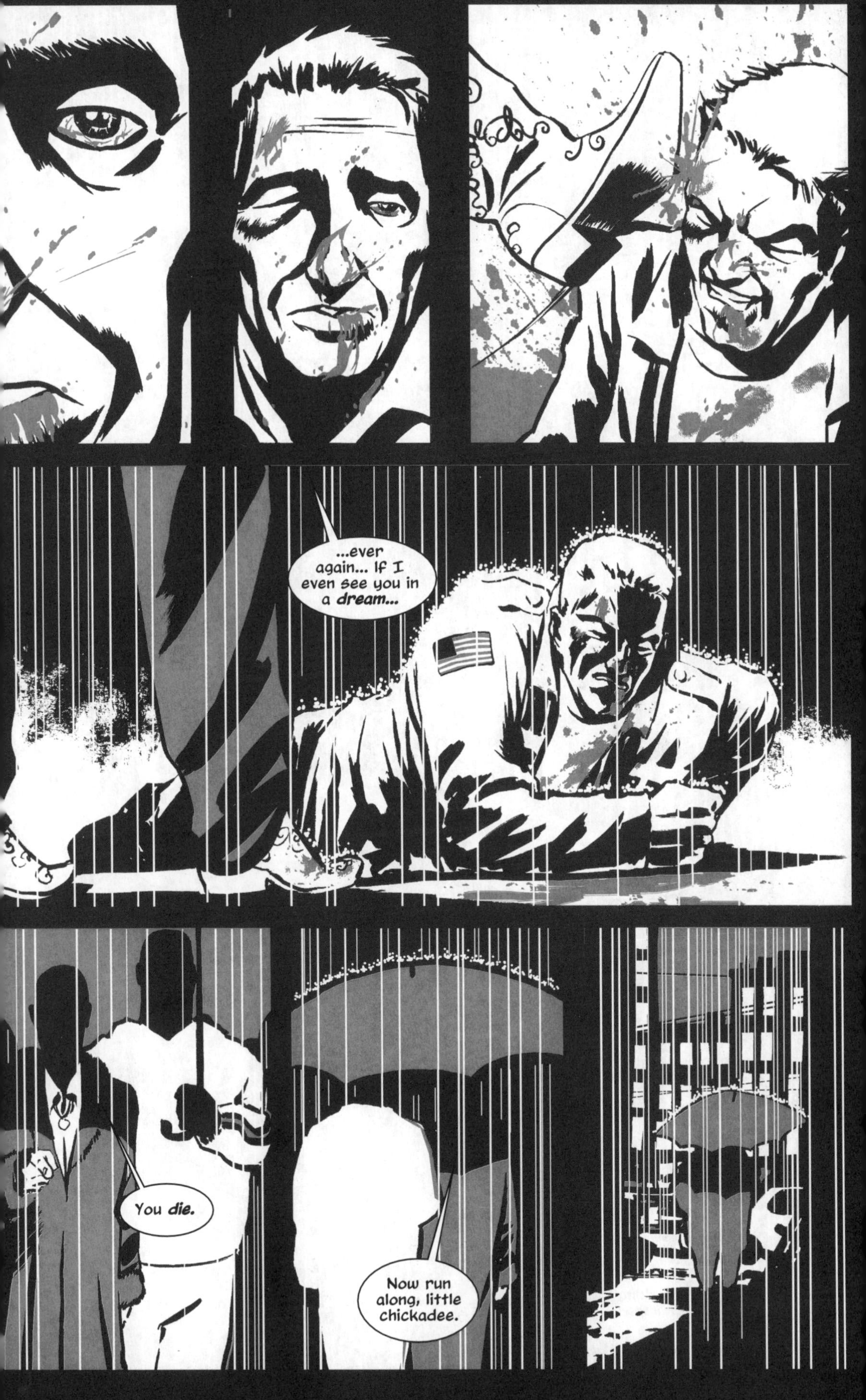
...ever again... If I even see you in a *dream*...
You *die.*
Now run along, little chickadee.

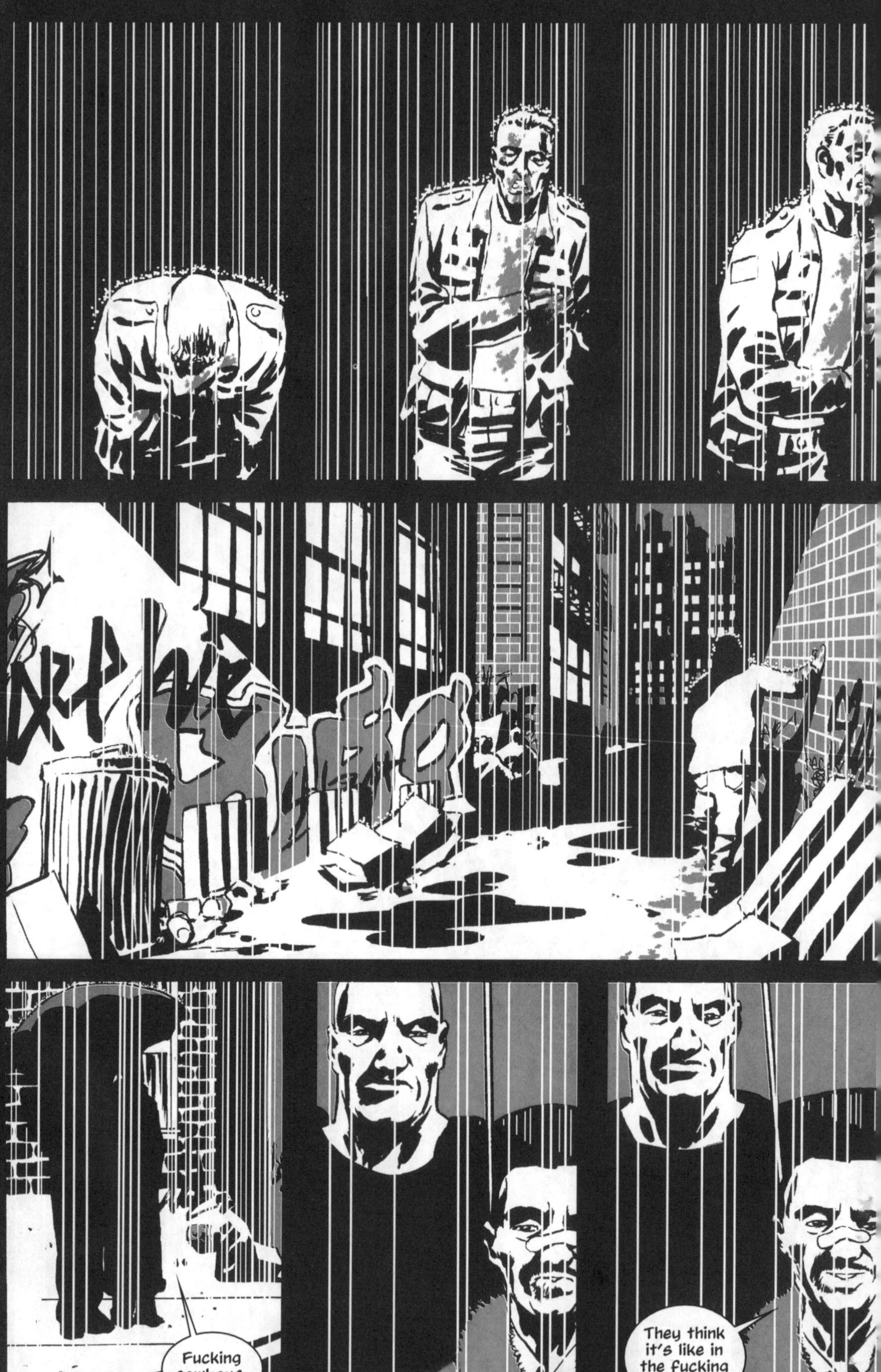
Fucking cowboys.
They think it's like in the fucking *movies*.

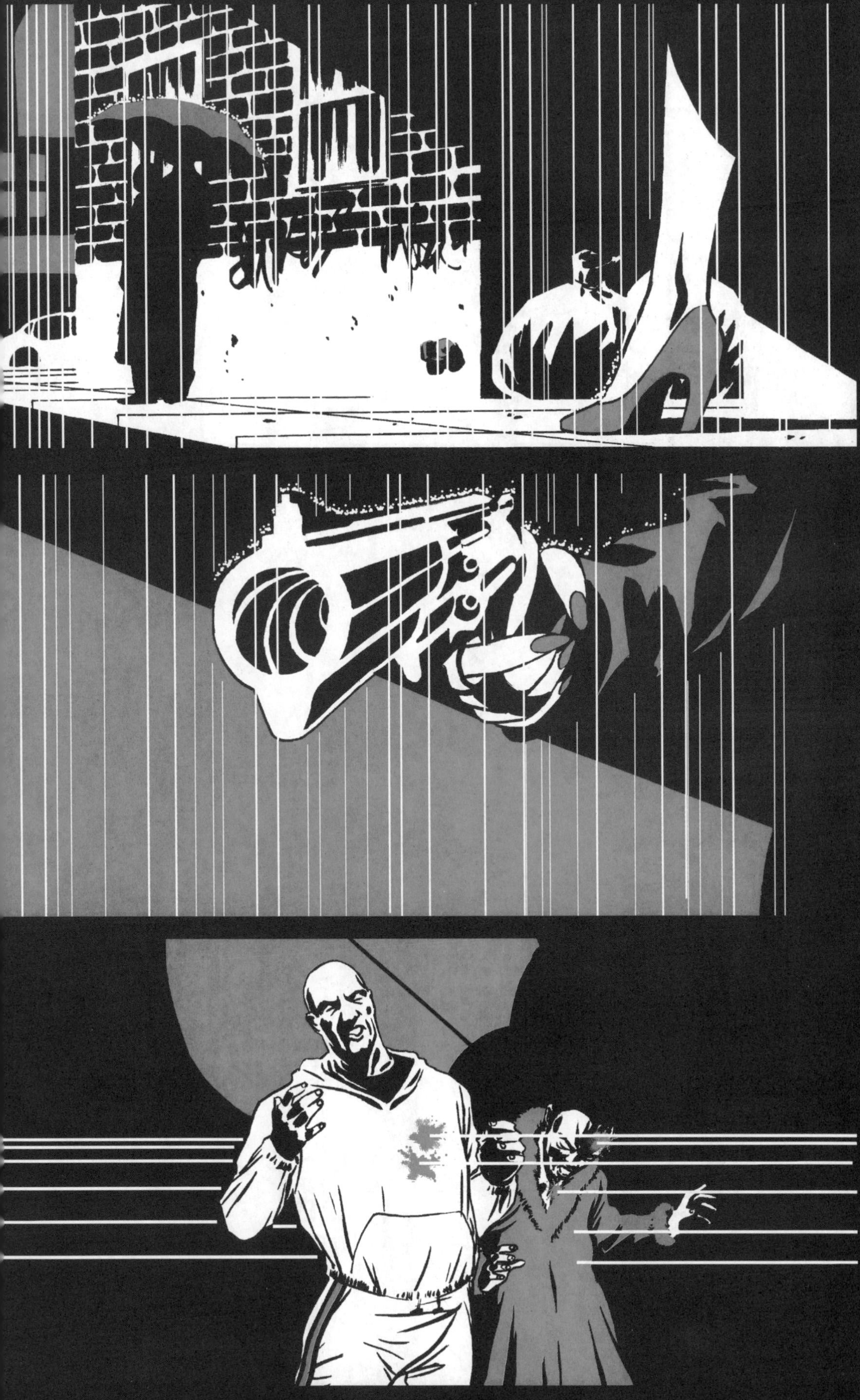

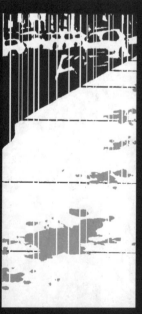

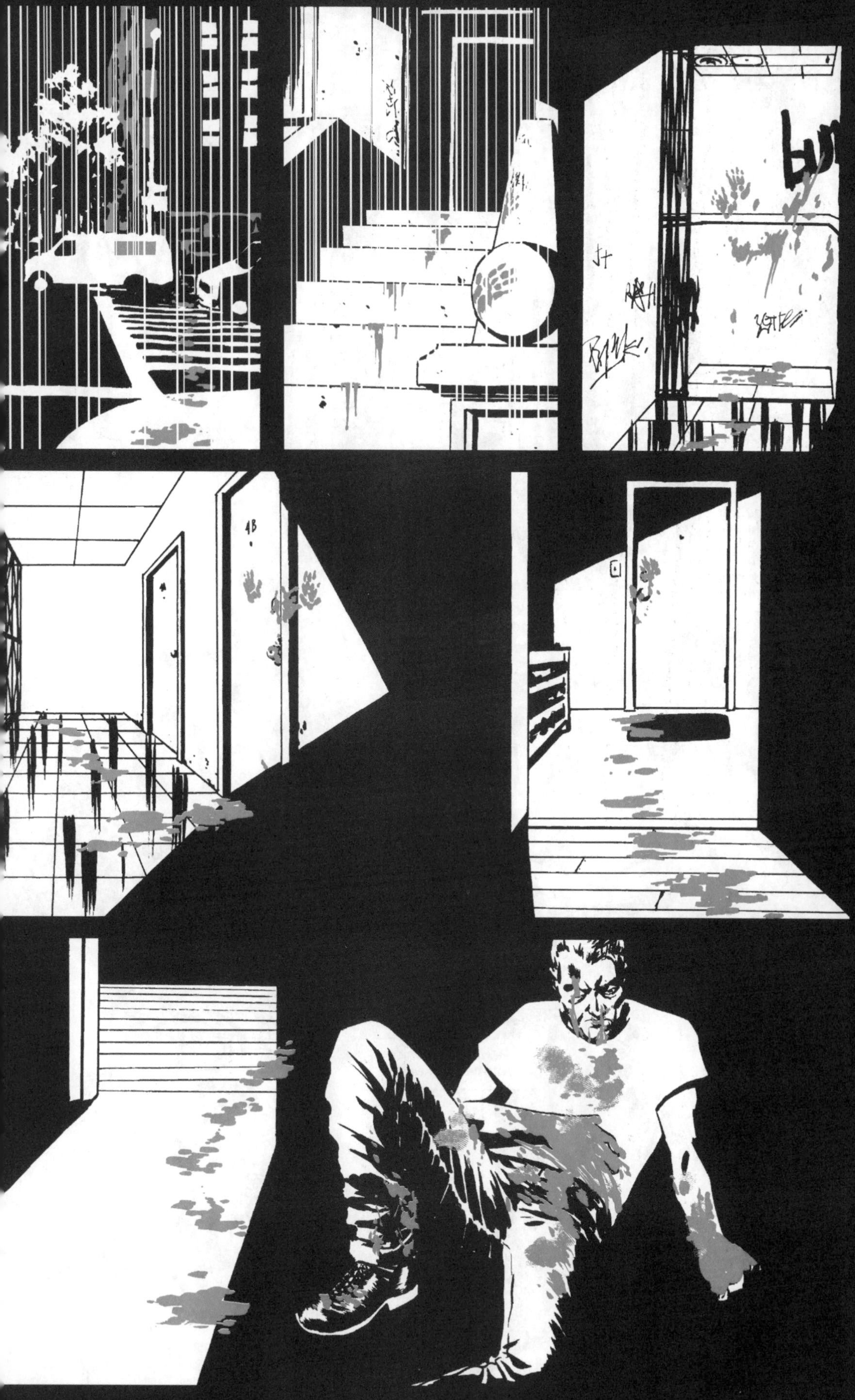
4B

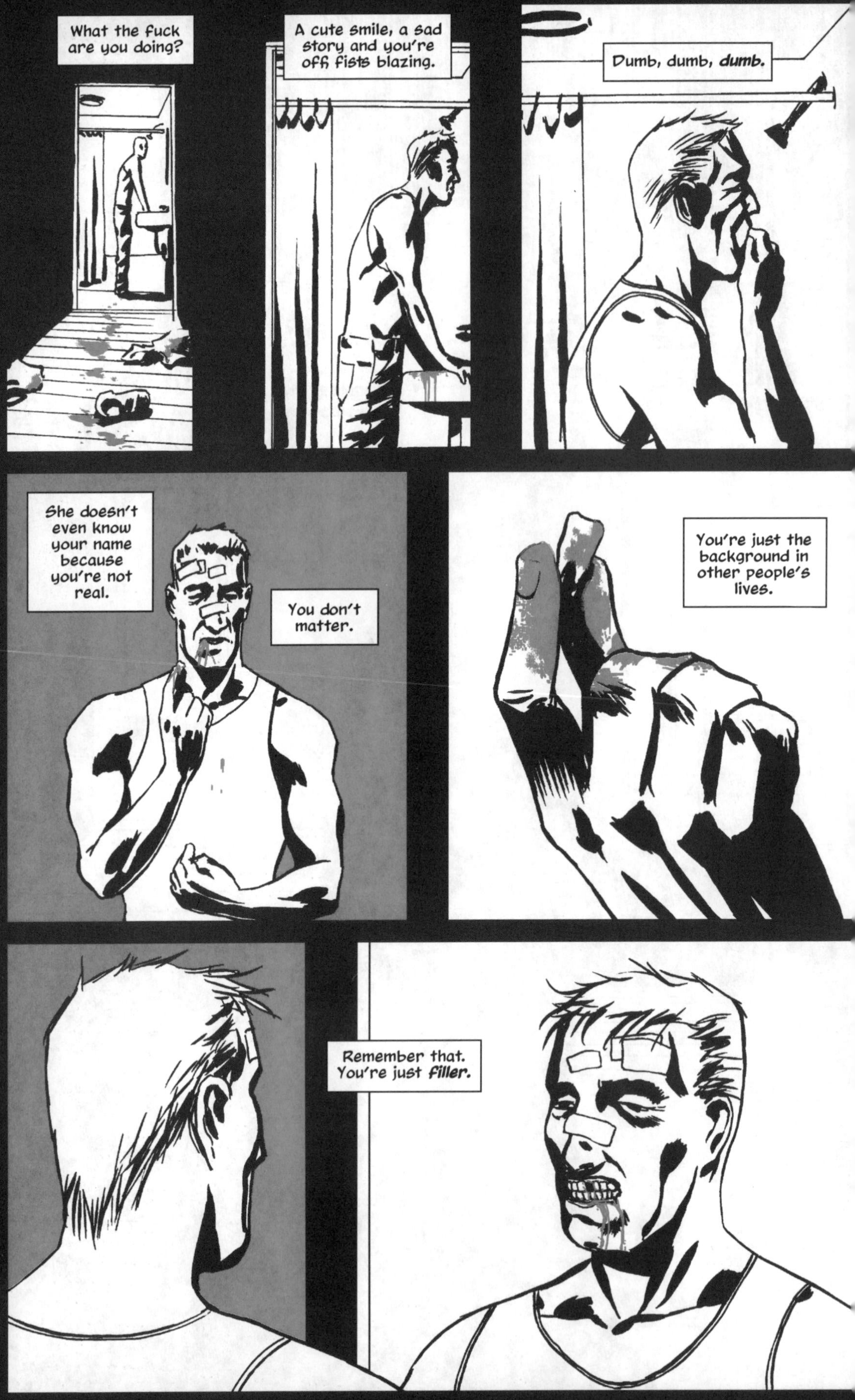
What the fuck are you doing?
A cute smile, a sad story and you're off fists blazing.
Dumb, dumb, *dumb.*
She doesn't even know your name because you're not real.
You don't matter.
You're just the background in other people's lives.
Remember that. You're just *filler.*

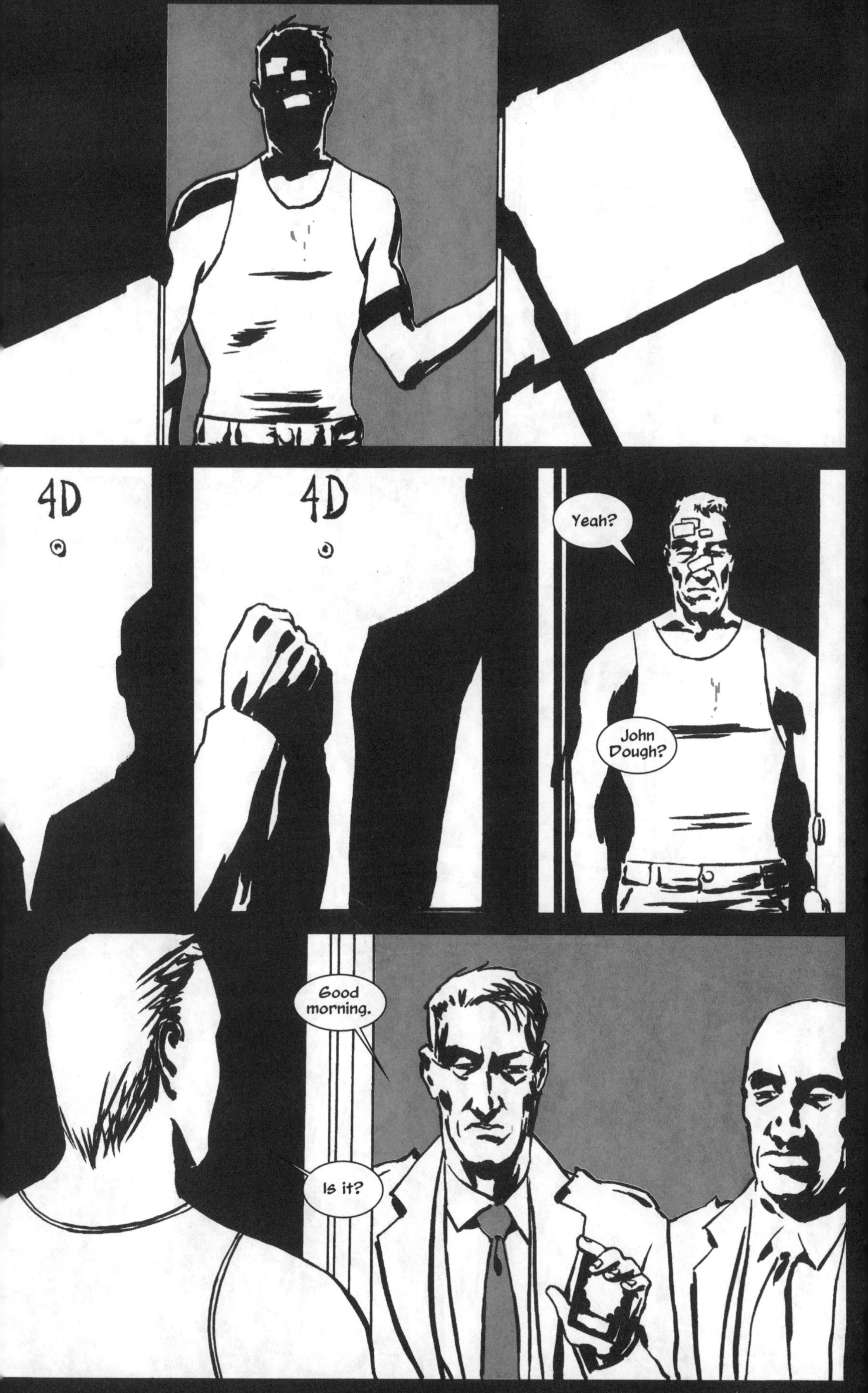
4D
4D
Yeah?
John Dough?
Good morning.
Is it?

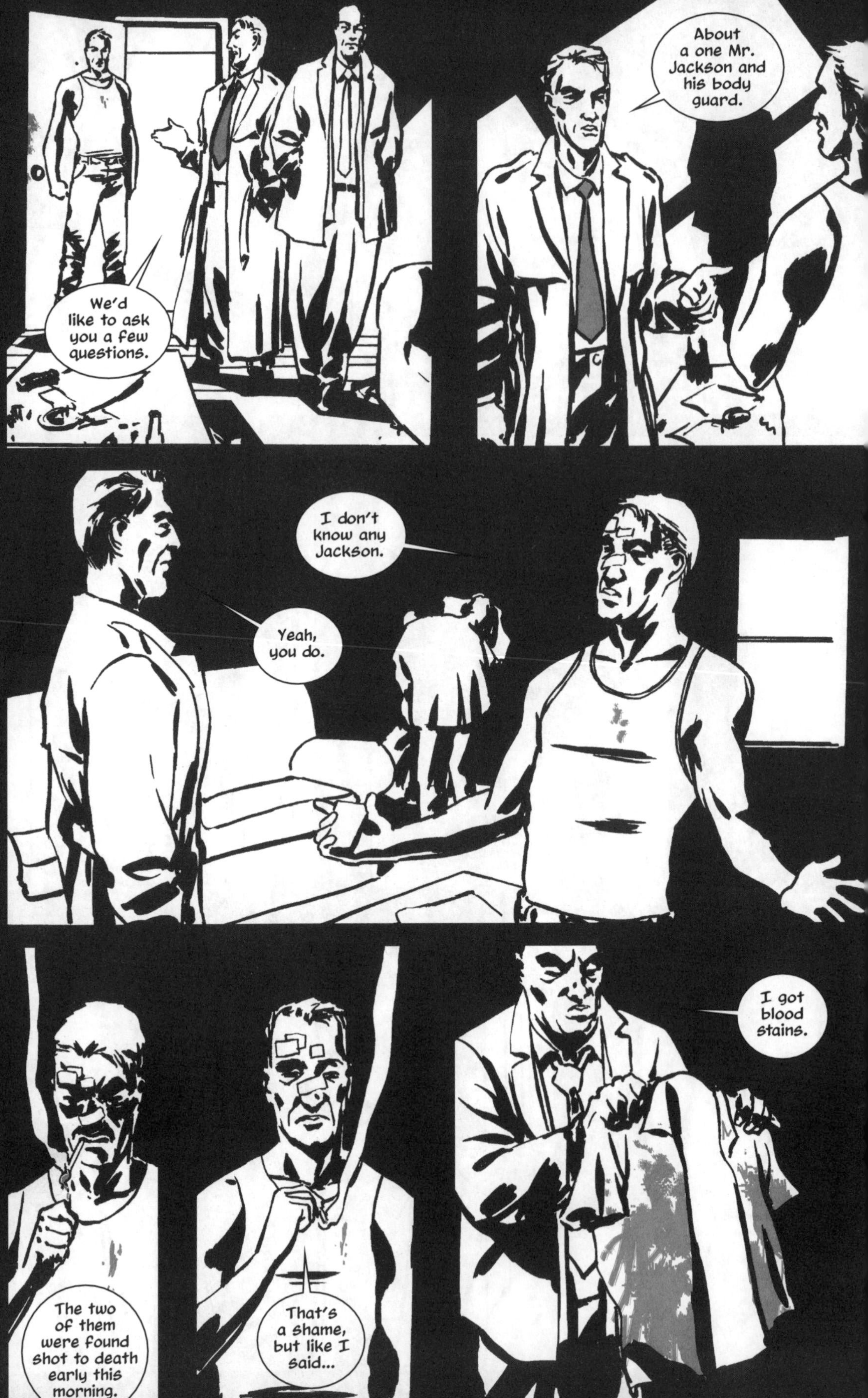
We'd like to ask you a few questions.
About a one Mr. Jackson and his body guard.
I don't know any Jackson.
Yeah, you do.
The two of them were found shot to death early this morning.
That's a shame, but like I said...
I got blood stains.

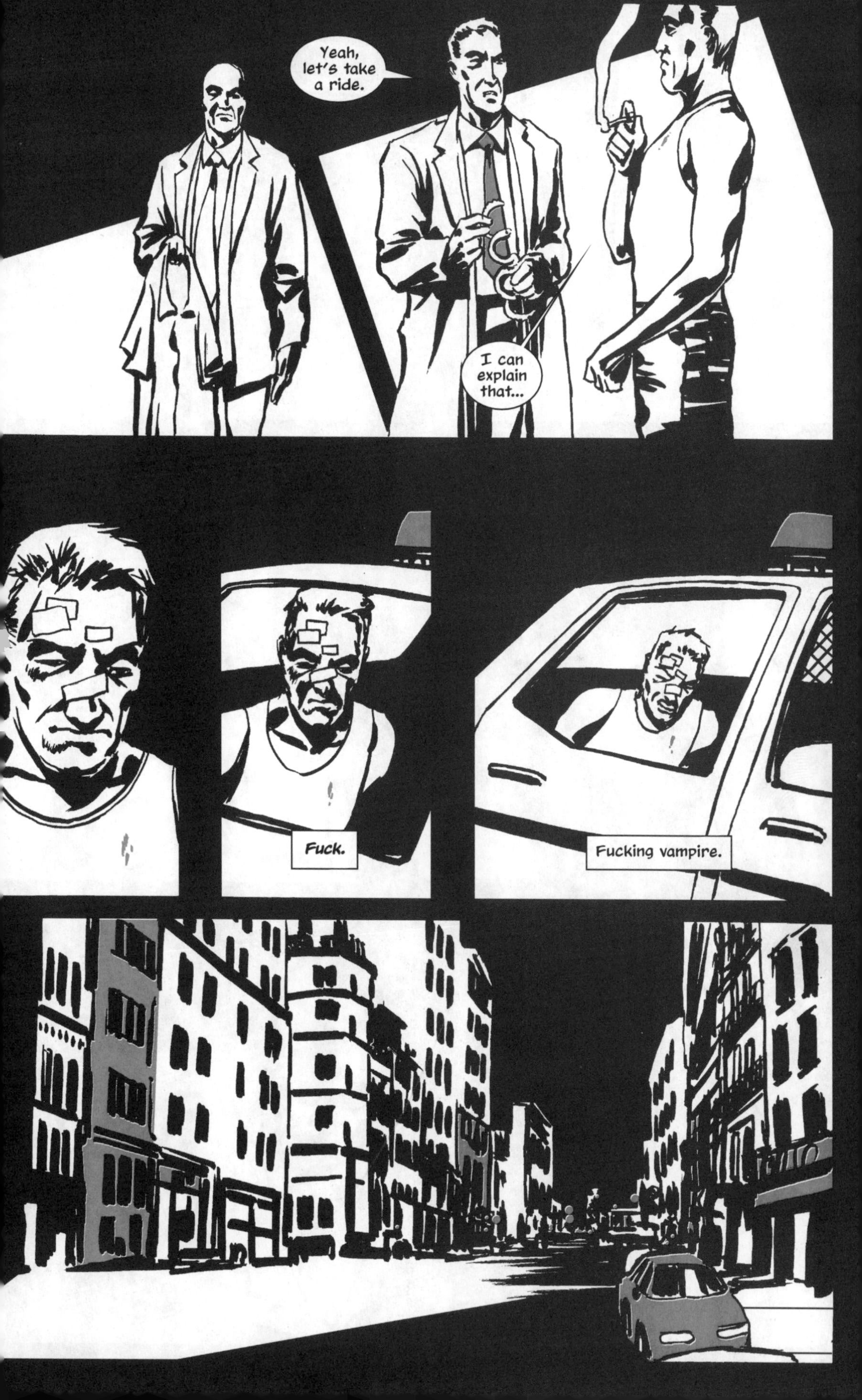
Yeah, let's take a ride.
I can explain that...
Fuck.
Fucking vampire.

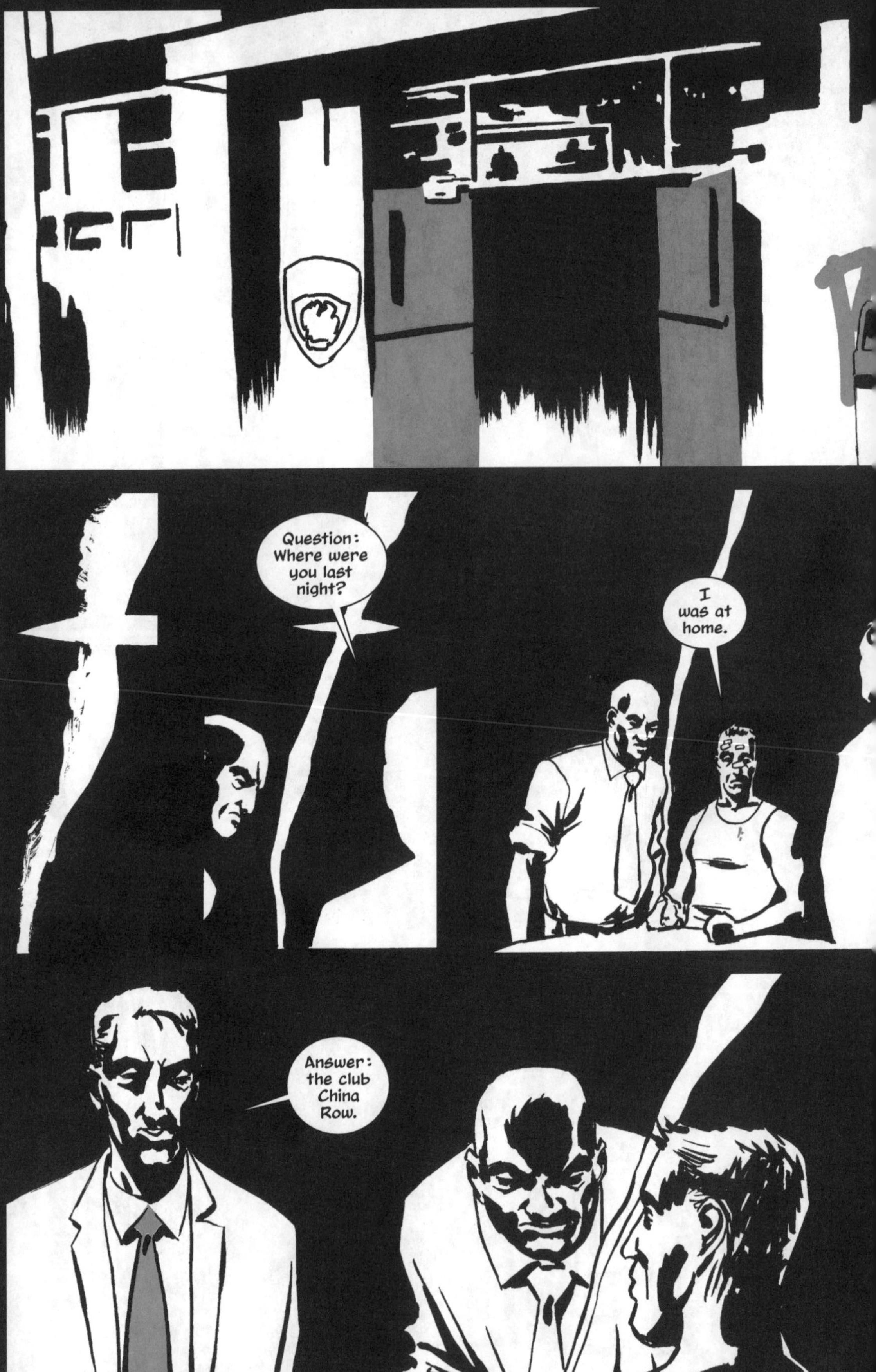
Question: Where were you last night?
I was at home.
Answer: the club China Row.

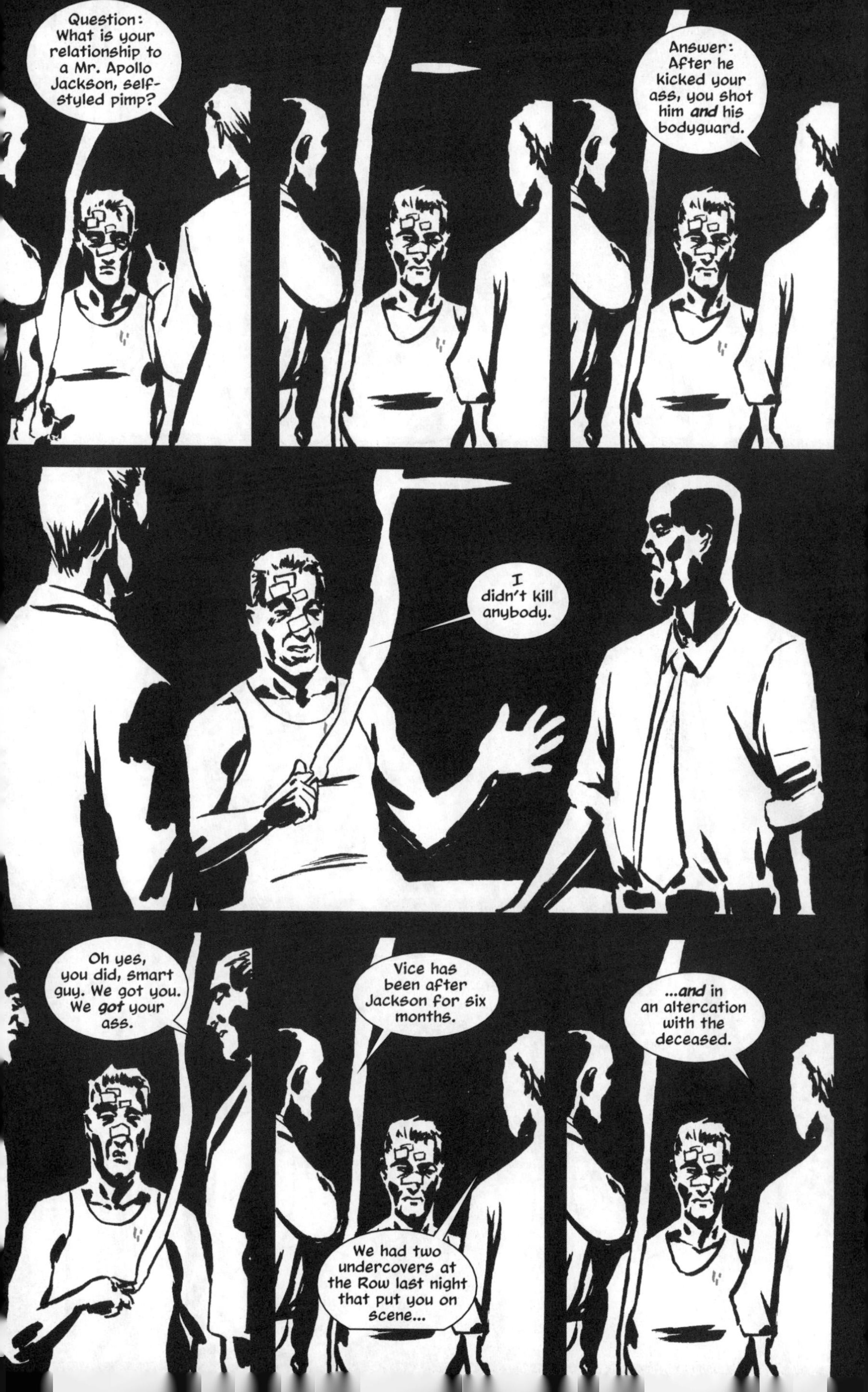
Question: What is your relationship to a Mr. Apollo Jackson, self-styled pimp?
Answer: After he kicked your ass, you shot him *and* his bodyguard.
I didn't kill anybody.
Oh yes, you did, smart guy. We got you. We *got* your ass.
Vice has been after Jackson for six months.
We had two undercovers at the Row last night that put you on scene...
...*and* in an altercation with the deceased.

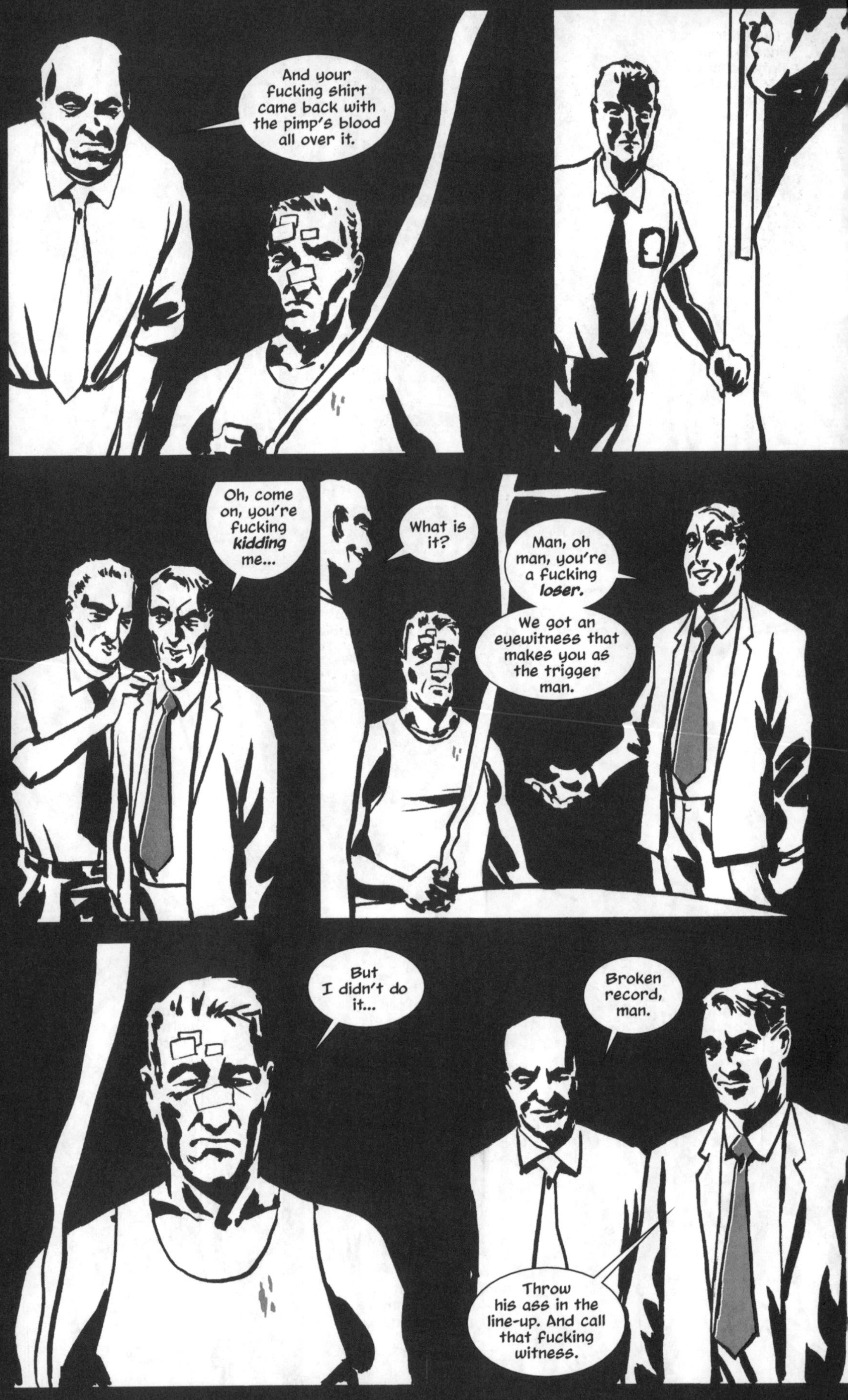
And your fucking shirt came back with the pimp's blood all over it.
Oh, come on, you're fucking *kidding* me...
What is it?
Man, oh man, you're a fucking *loser.*
We got an eyewitness that makes you as the trigger man.
But I didn't do it...
Broken record, man.
Throw his ass in the line-up. And call that fucking witness.

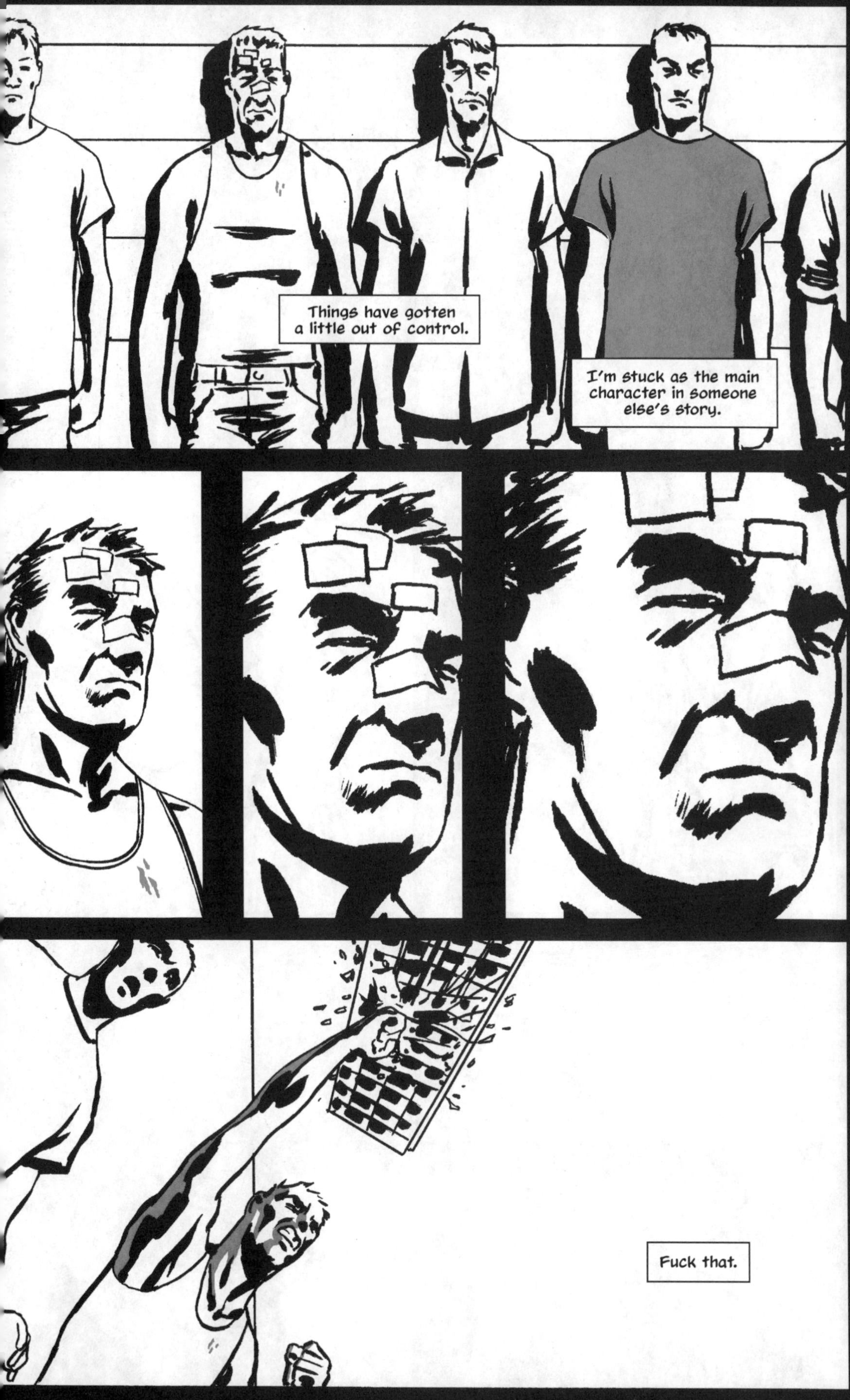
Things have gotten a little out of control.
I'm stuck as the main character in someone else's story.
Fuck that.

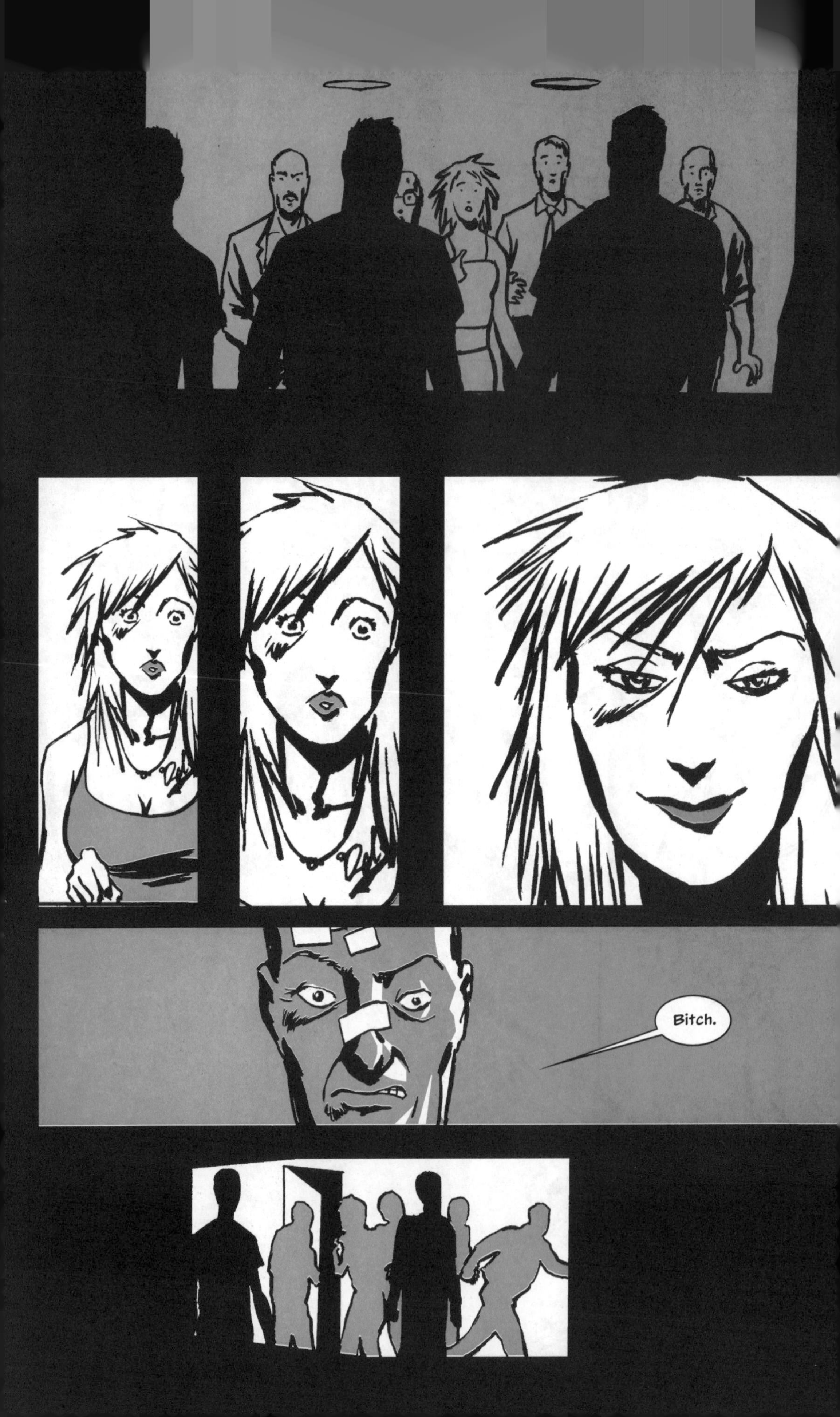
Bitch.

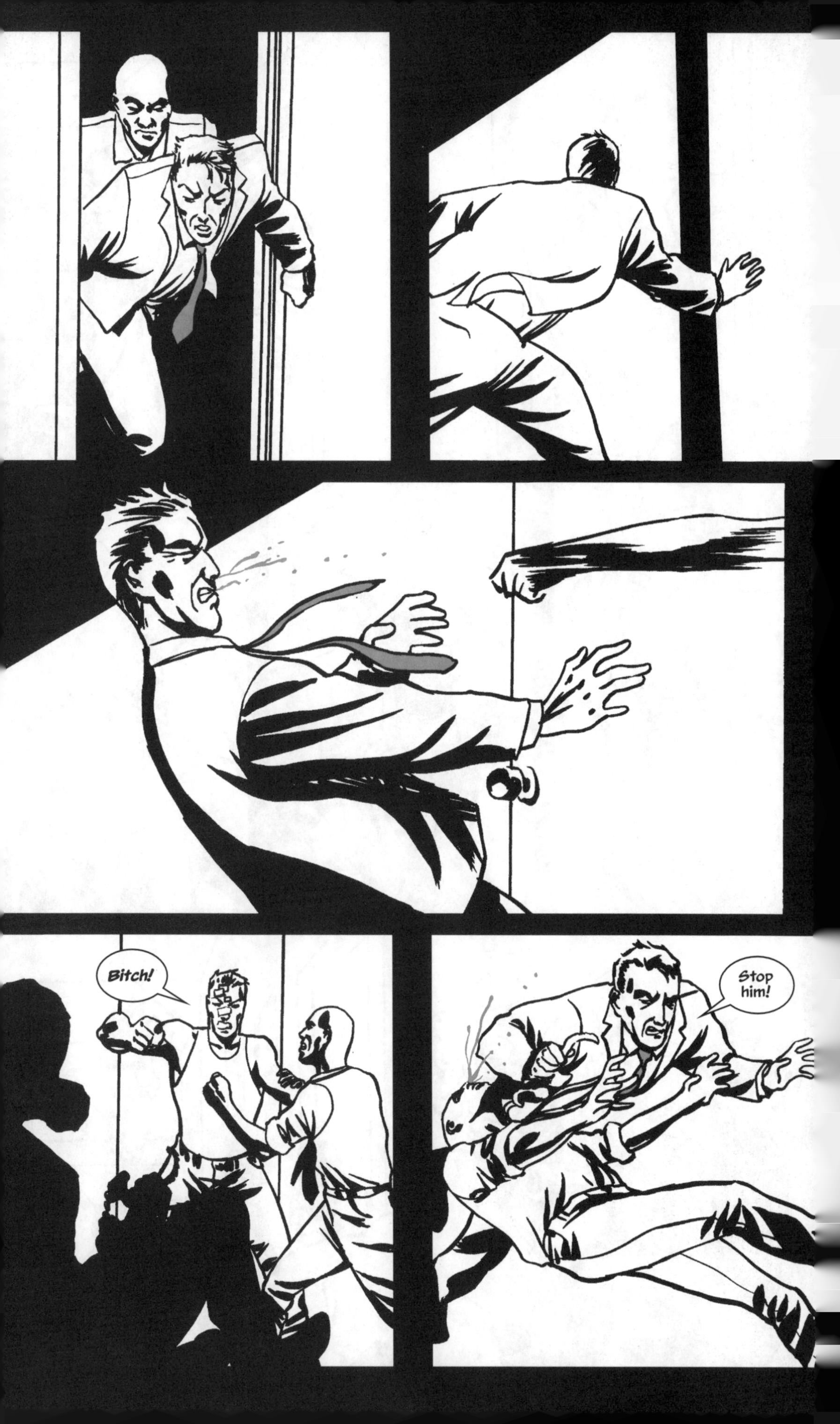
Bitch!
Stop him!

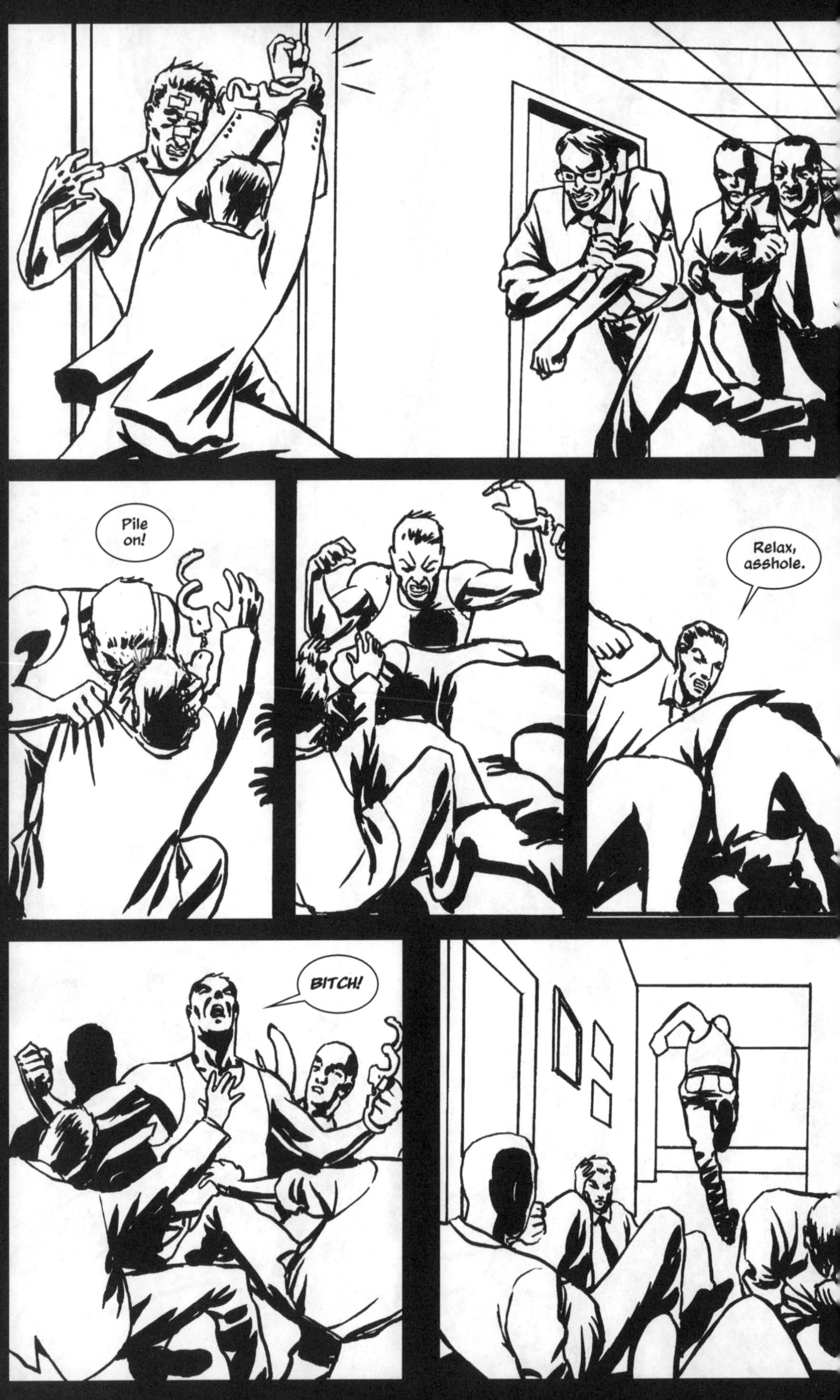
Pile on!
Relax, asshole.
BITCH!

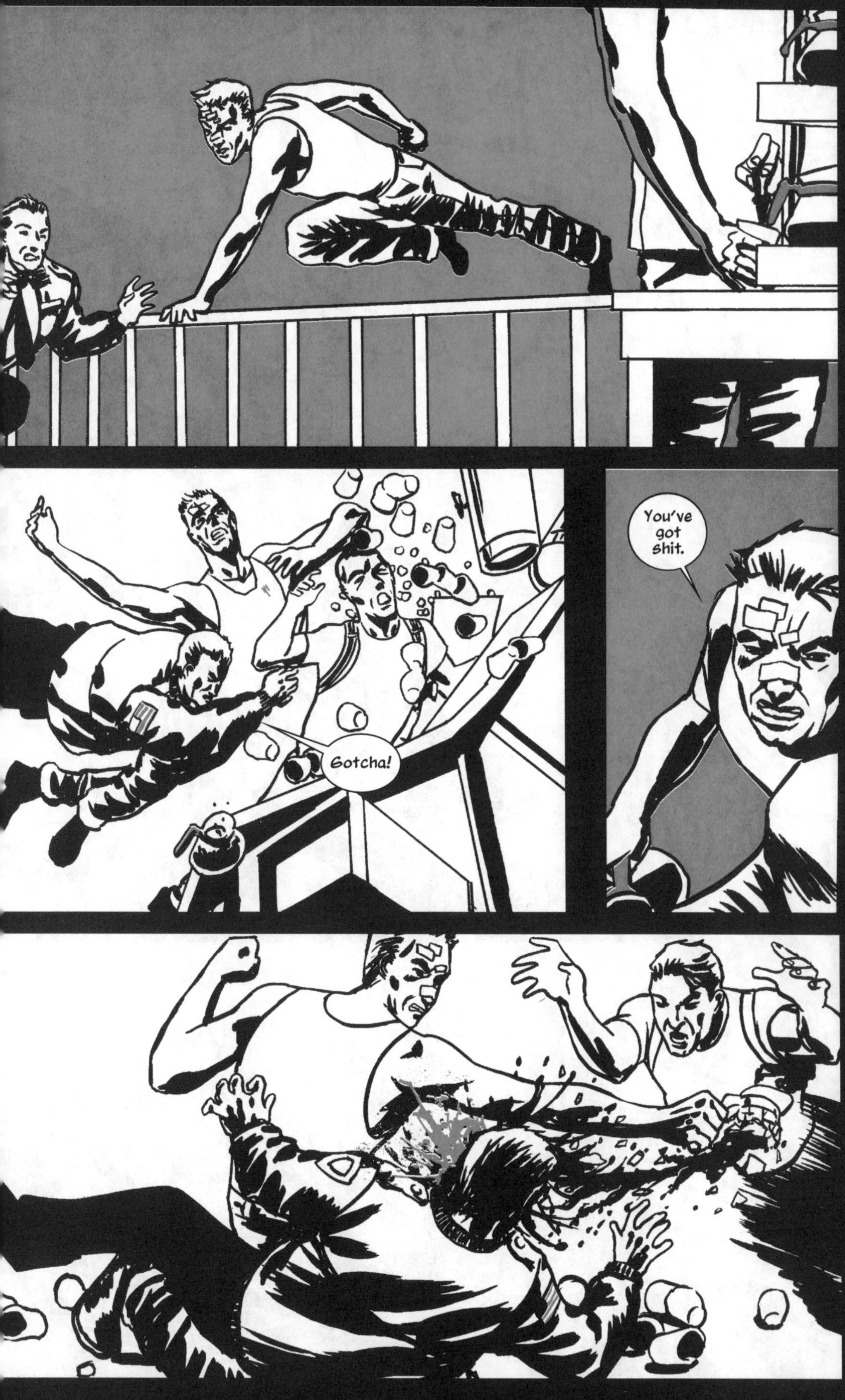
Gotcha!
You've got shit.

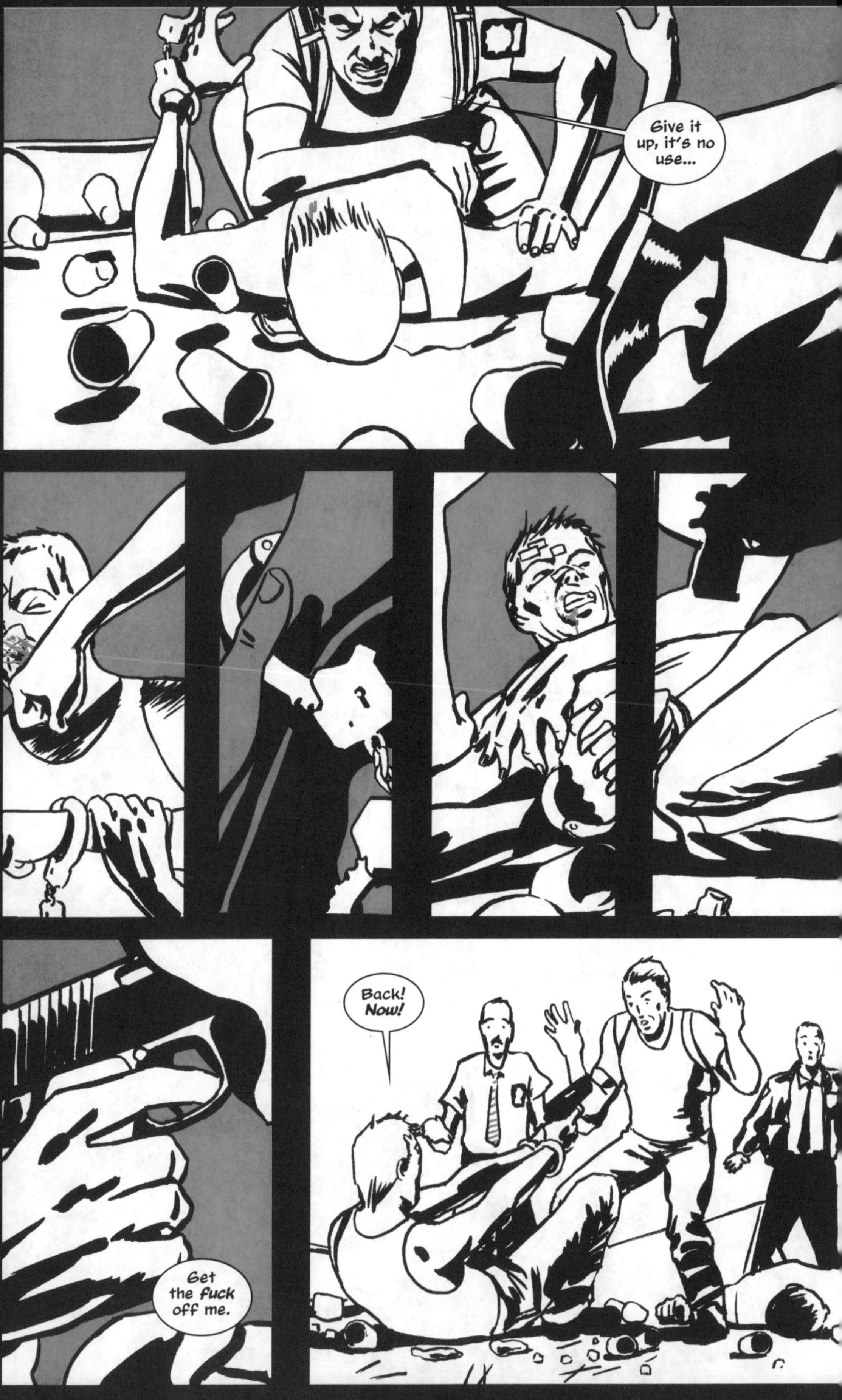
Give it up, it's no use...
Get the fuck off me.
Back! Now!

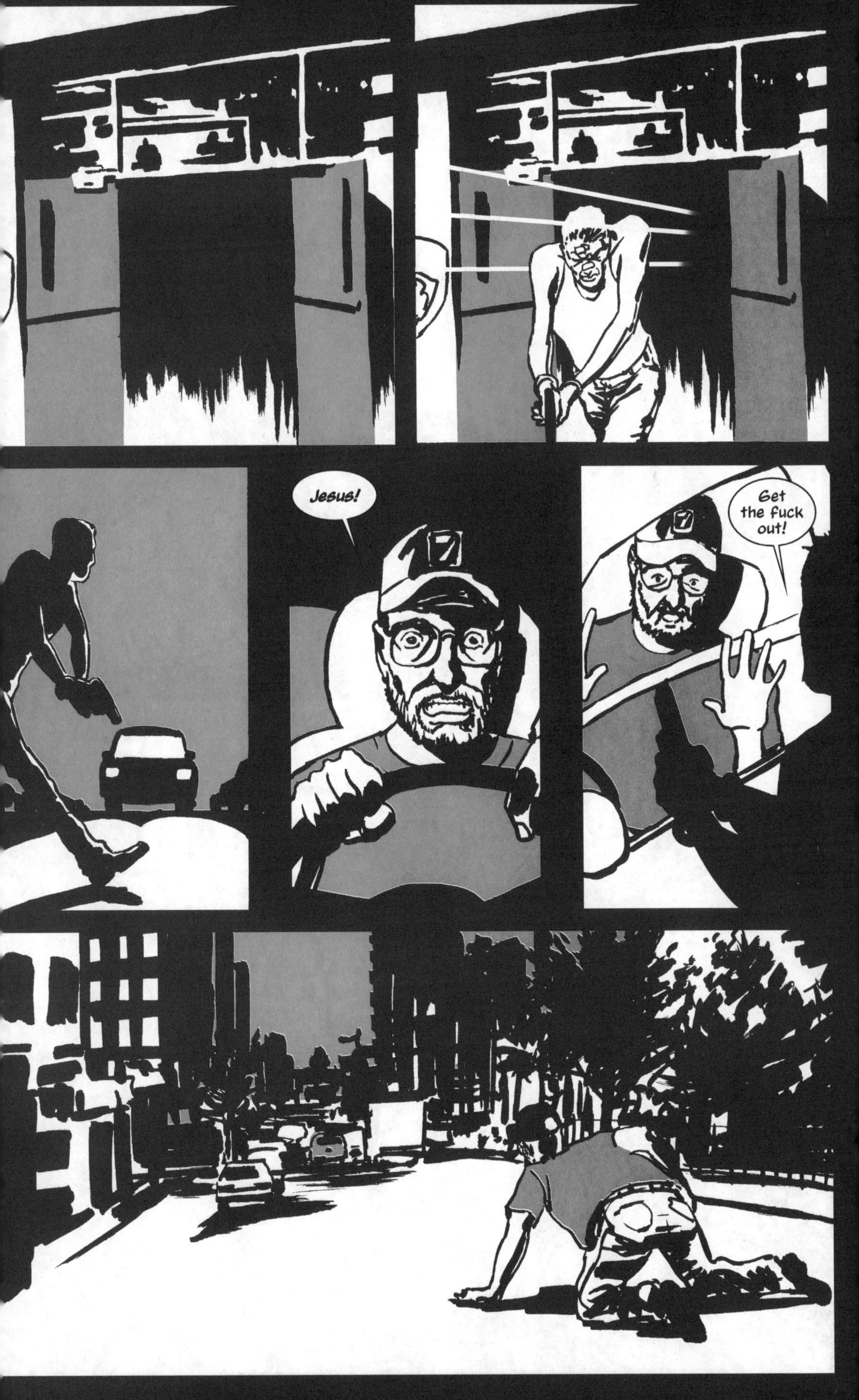
Jesus!
Get the fuck out!

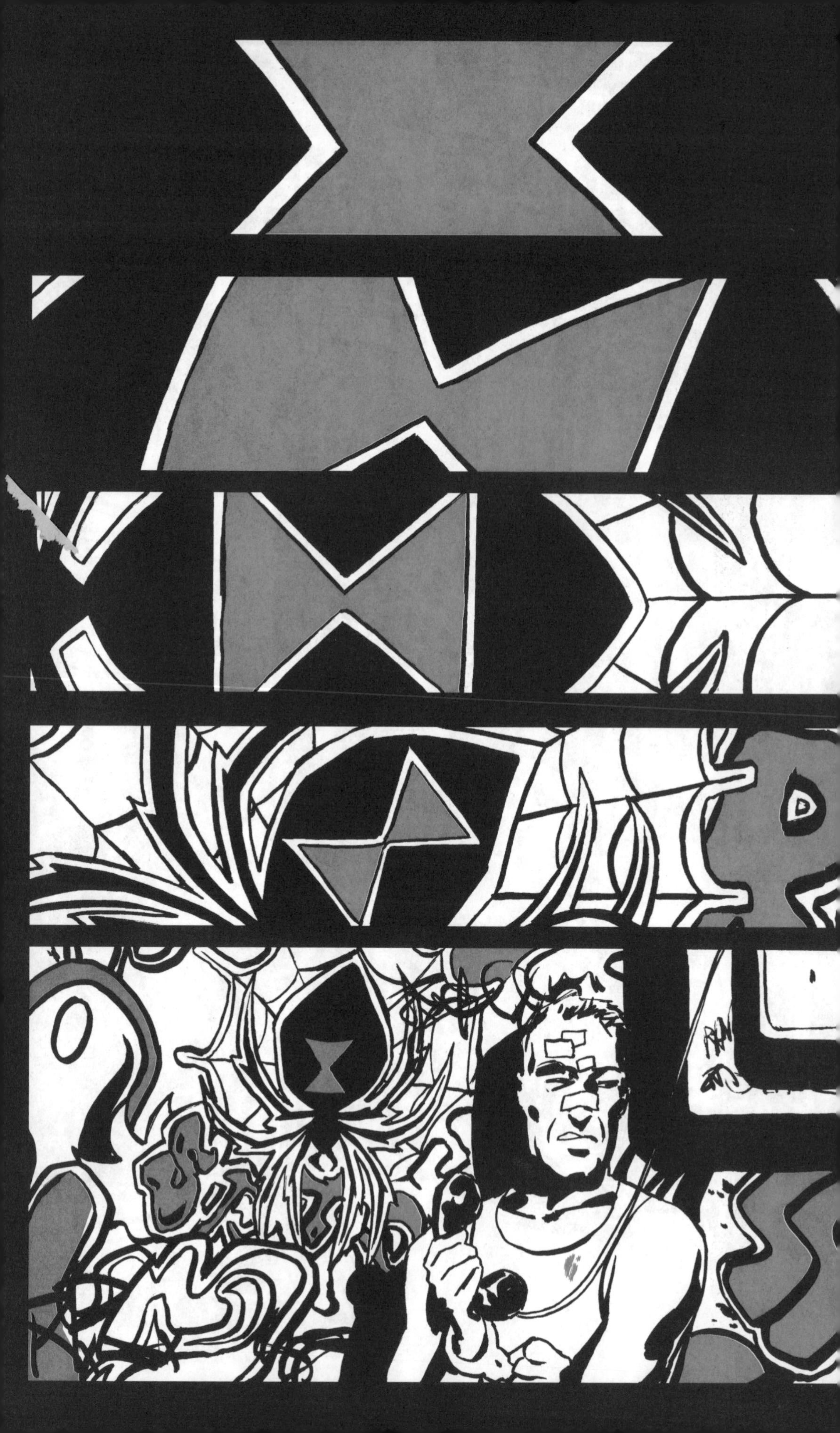

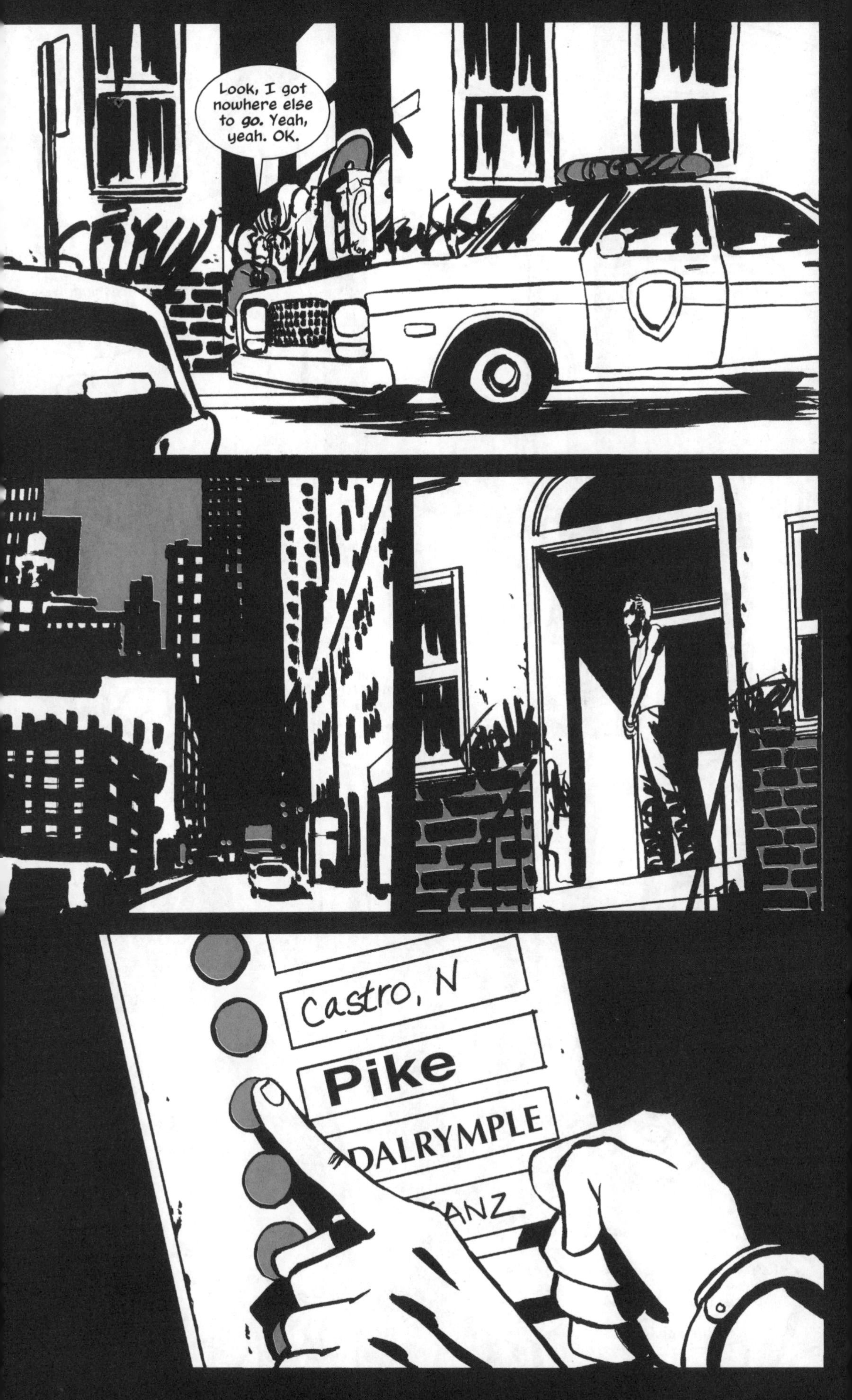
Look, I got nowhere else to go. Yeah, yeah. OK.
Castro, N
Pike
DALRYMPLE

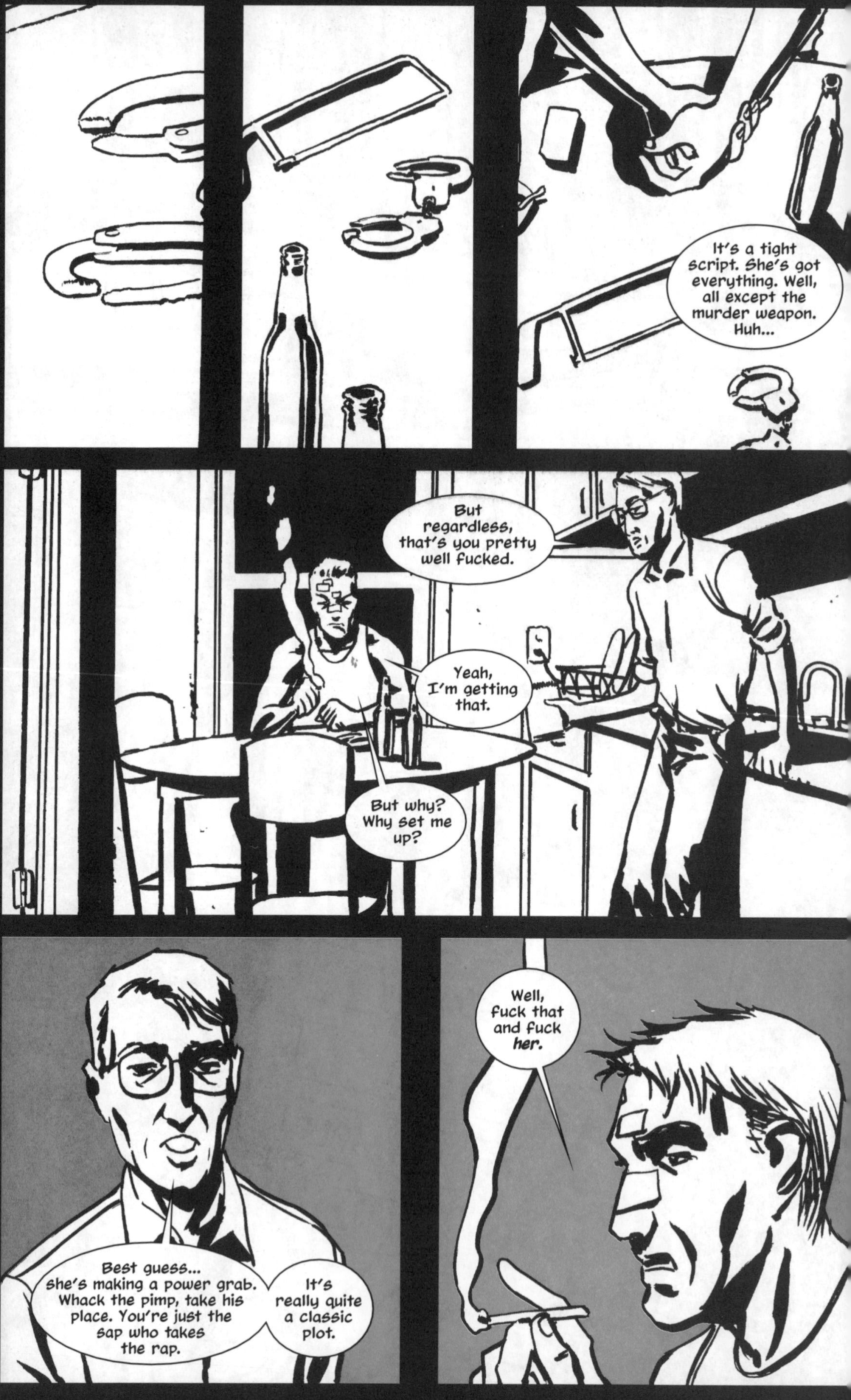
It's a tight script. She's got everything. Well, all except the murder weapon. Huh...
But regardless, that's you pretty well fucked.
Yeah, I'm getting that.
But why? Why set me up?
Best guess... she's making a power grab. Whack the pimp, take his place. You're just the sap who takes the rap.
It's really quite a classic plot.
Well, fuck that and fuck *her*.

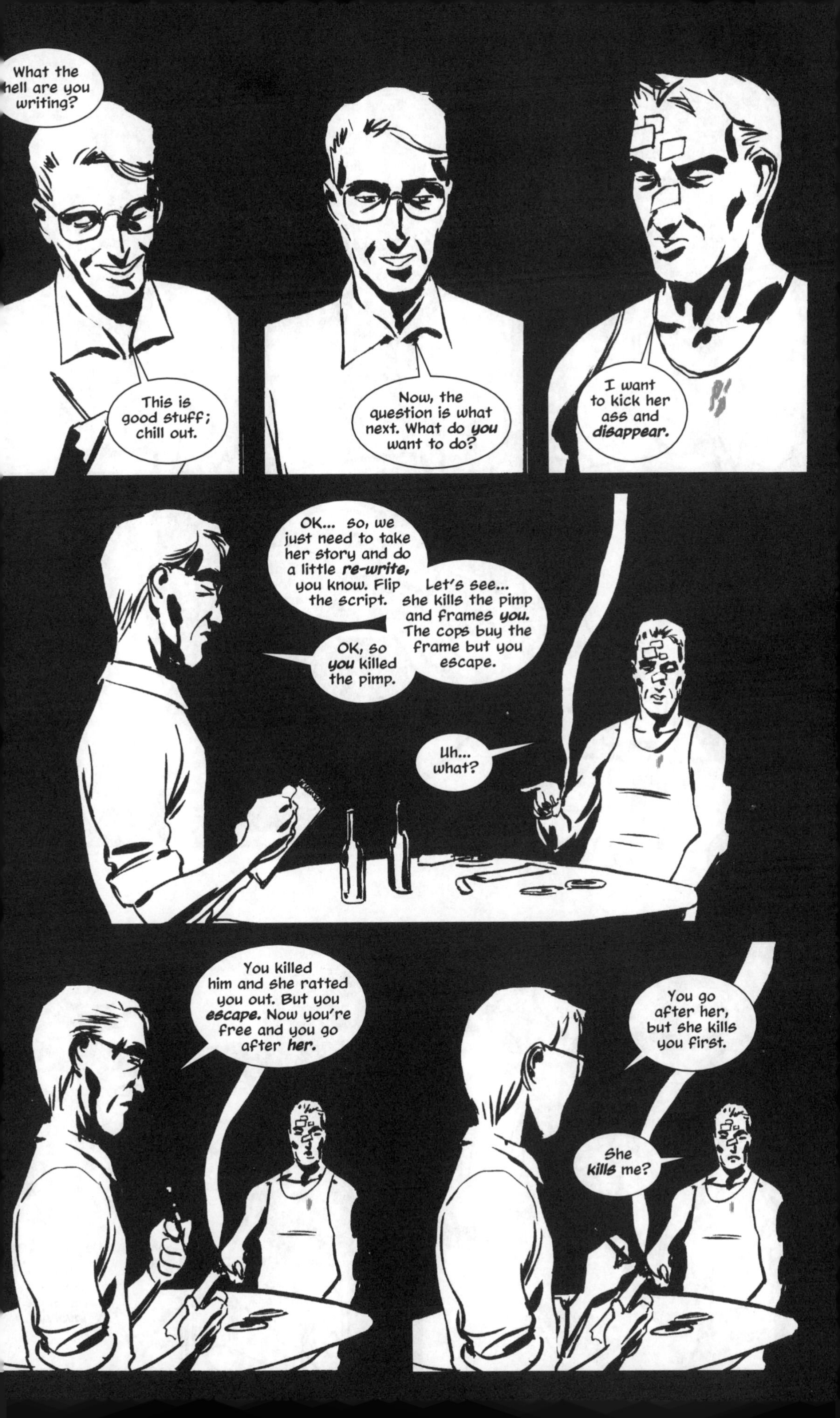
What the hell are you writing?
This is good stuff; chill out.
Now, the question is what next. What do *you* want to do?
I want to kick her ass and ***disappear.***
OK... so, we just need to take her story and do a little ***re-write,*** you know. Flip the script.
Let's see... she kills the pimp and frames ***you.*** The cops buy the frame but you escape.
OK, so ***you*** killed the pimp.
Uh... what?
You killed him and she ratted you out. But you ***escape.*** Now you're free and you go after ***her.***
You go after her, but she kills you first.
She ***kills*** me?

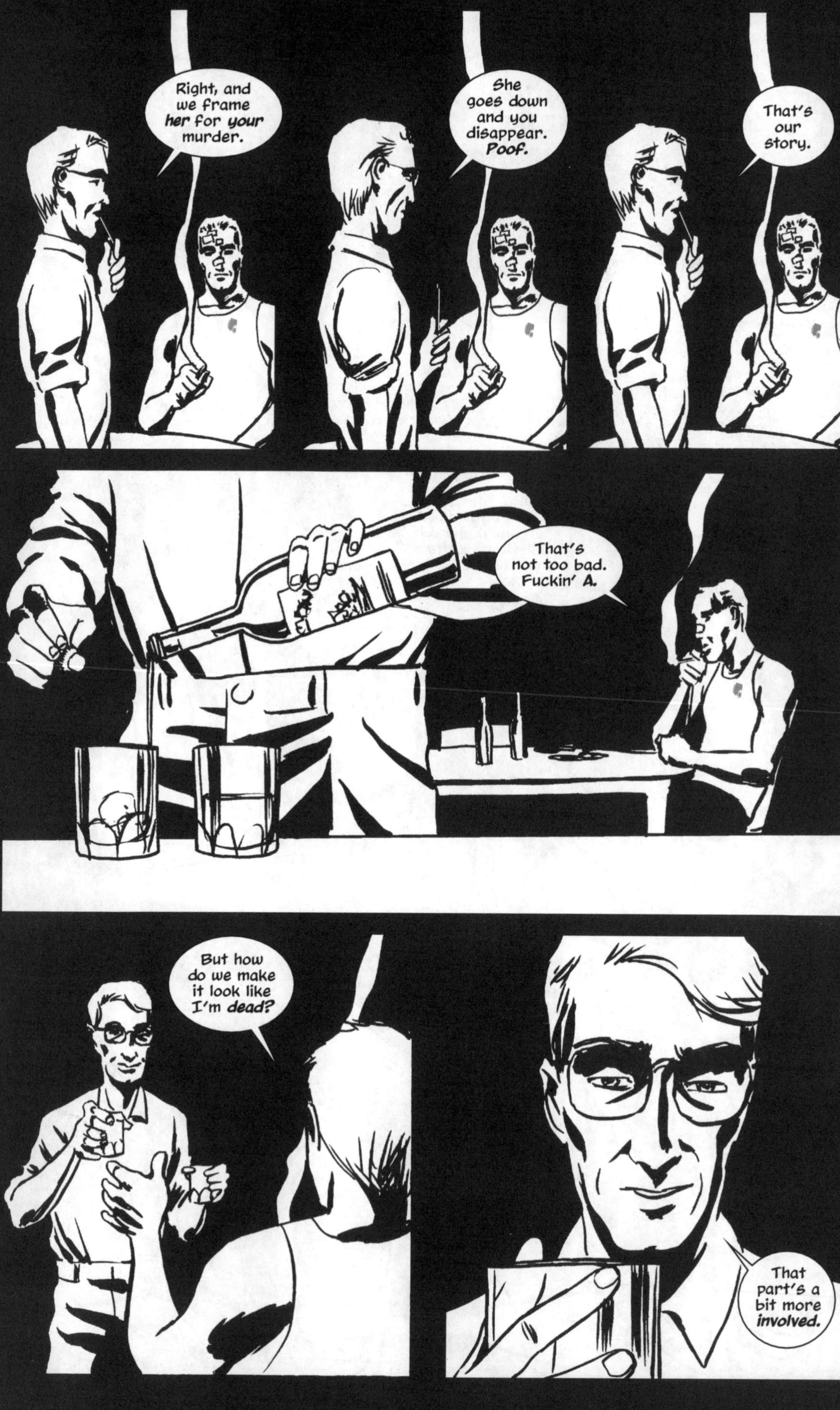
Right, and we frame her for your murder.
She goes down and you disappear. Poof.
That's our story.
That's not too bad. Fuckin' A.
But how do we make it look like I'm dead?
That part's a bit more involved.

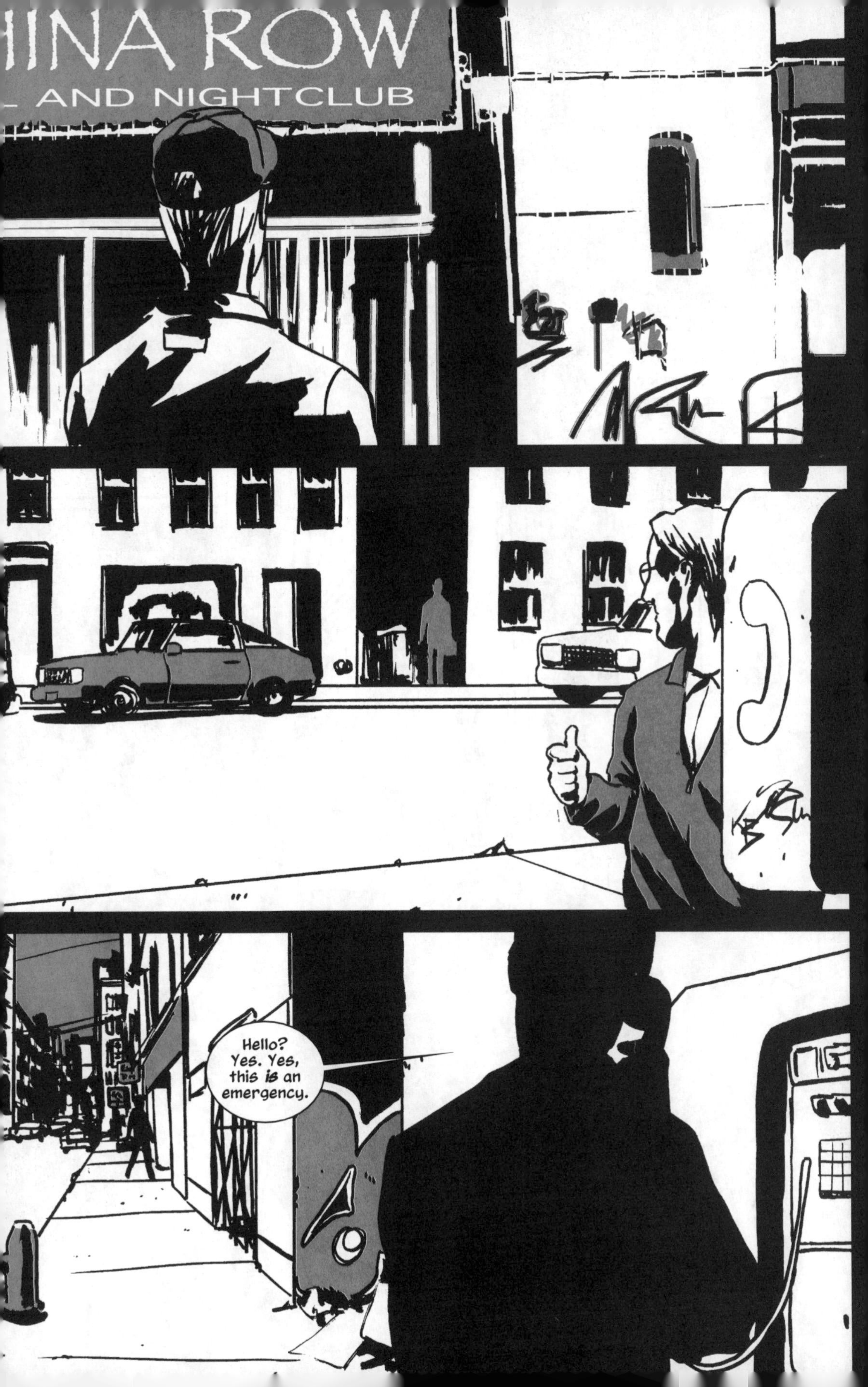
HINA ROW
L AND NIGHTCLUB
Hello? Yes. Yes, this *is* an emergency.

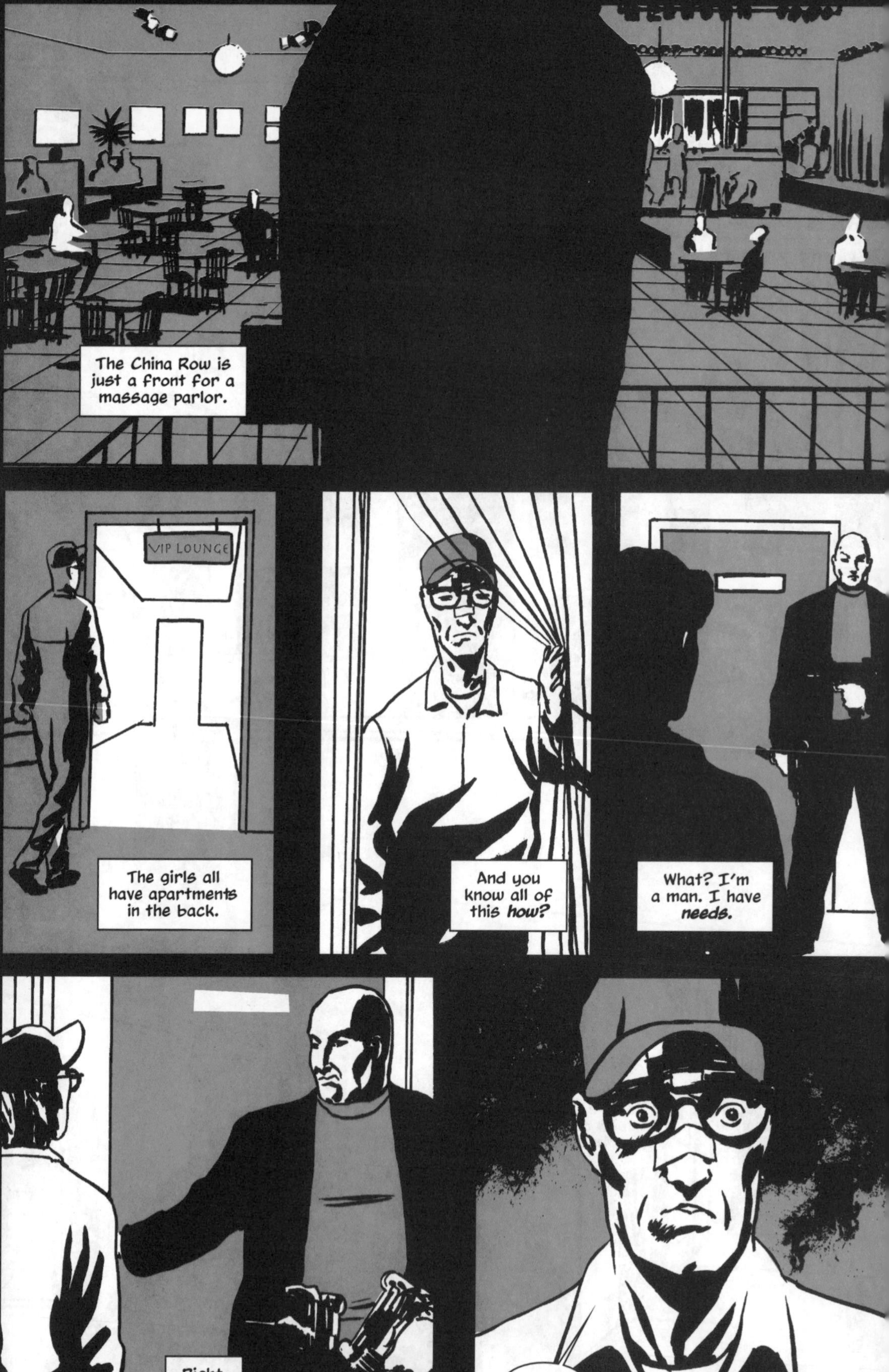
The China Row is just a front for a massage parlor.
VIP LOUNGE
The girls all have apartments in the back.
And you know all of this *how?*
What? I'm a man. I have *needs.*
Right.
Jesus.

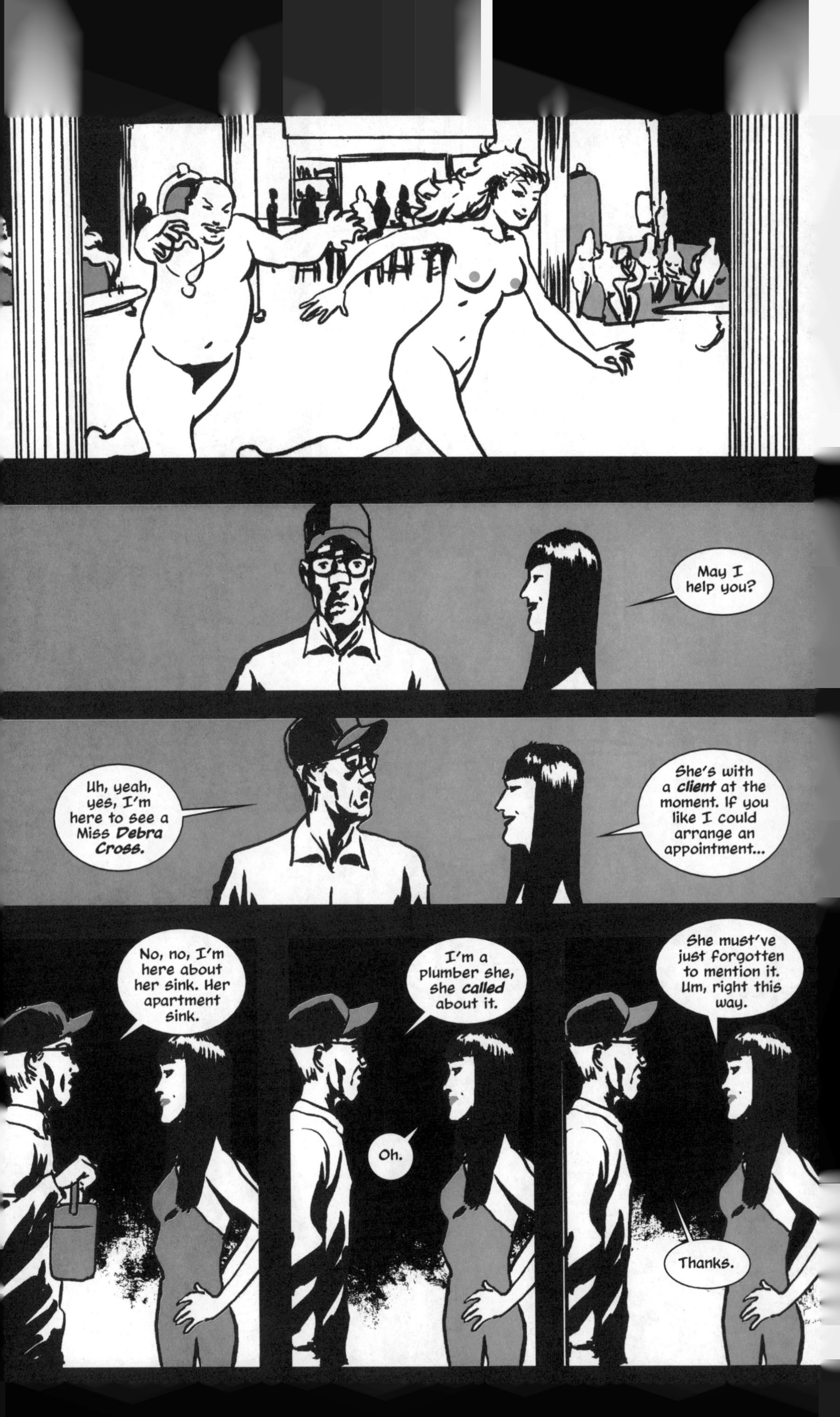
May I help you?
Uh, yeah, yes, I'm here to see a Miss *Debra Cross.*
She's with a *client* at the moment. If you like I could arrange an appointment...
No, no, I'm here about her sink. Her apartment sink.
I'm a plumber she, she *called* about it.
Oh.
She must've just forgotten to mention it. Um, right this way.
Thanks.

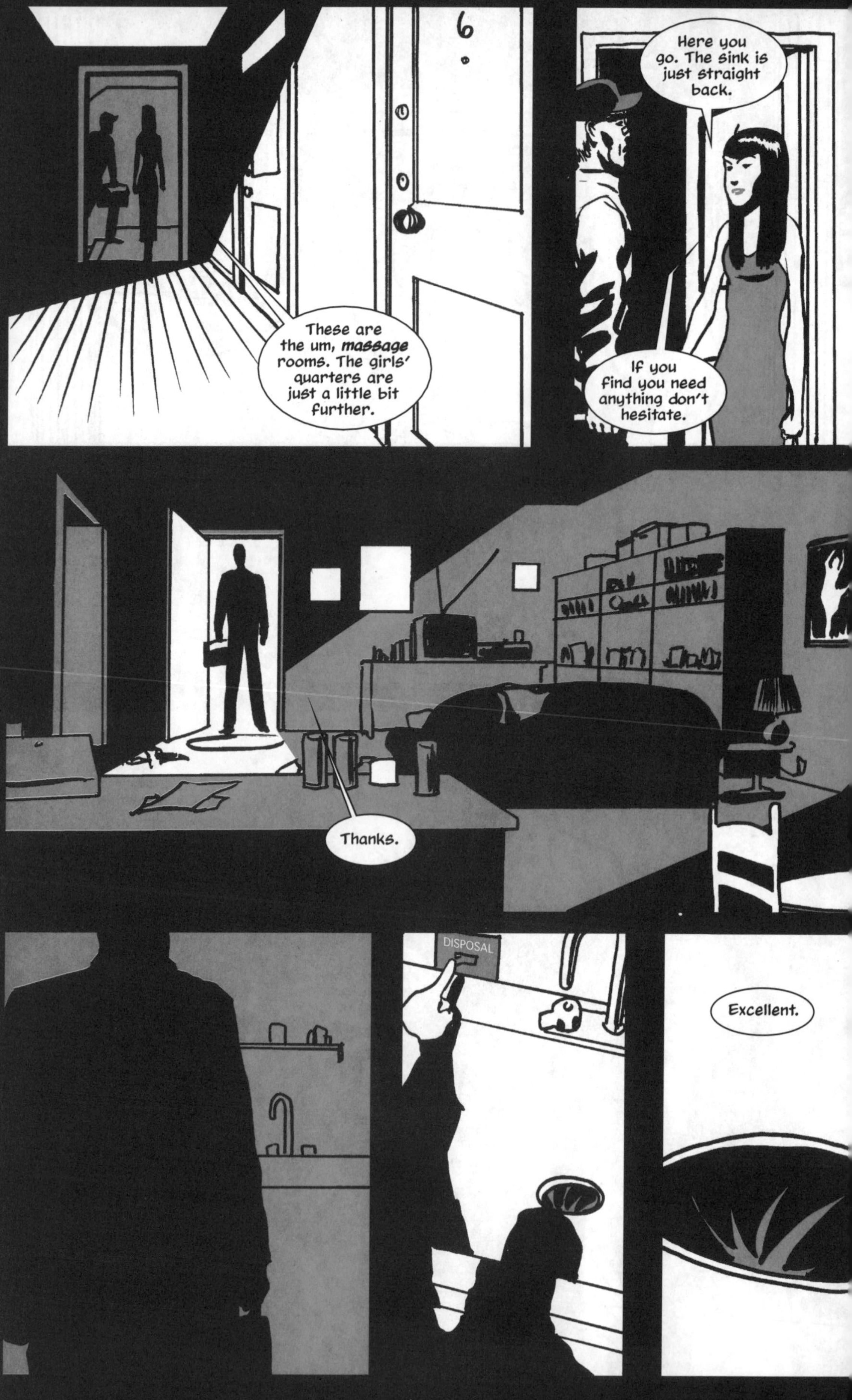
These are the um, *massage* rooms. The girls' quarters are just a little bit further.
Here you go. The sink is just straight back.
If you find you need anything don't hesitate.
Thanks.
DISPOSAL
Excellent.

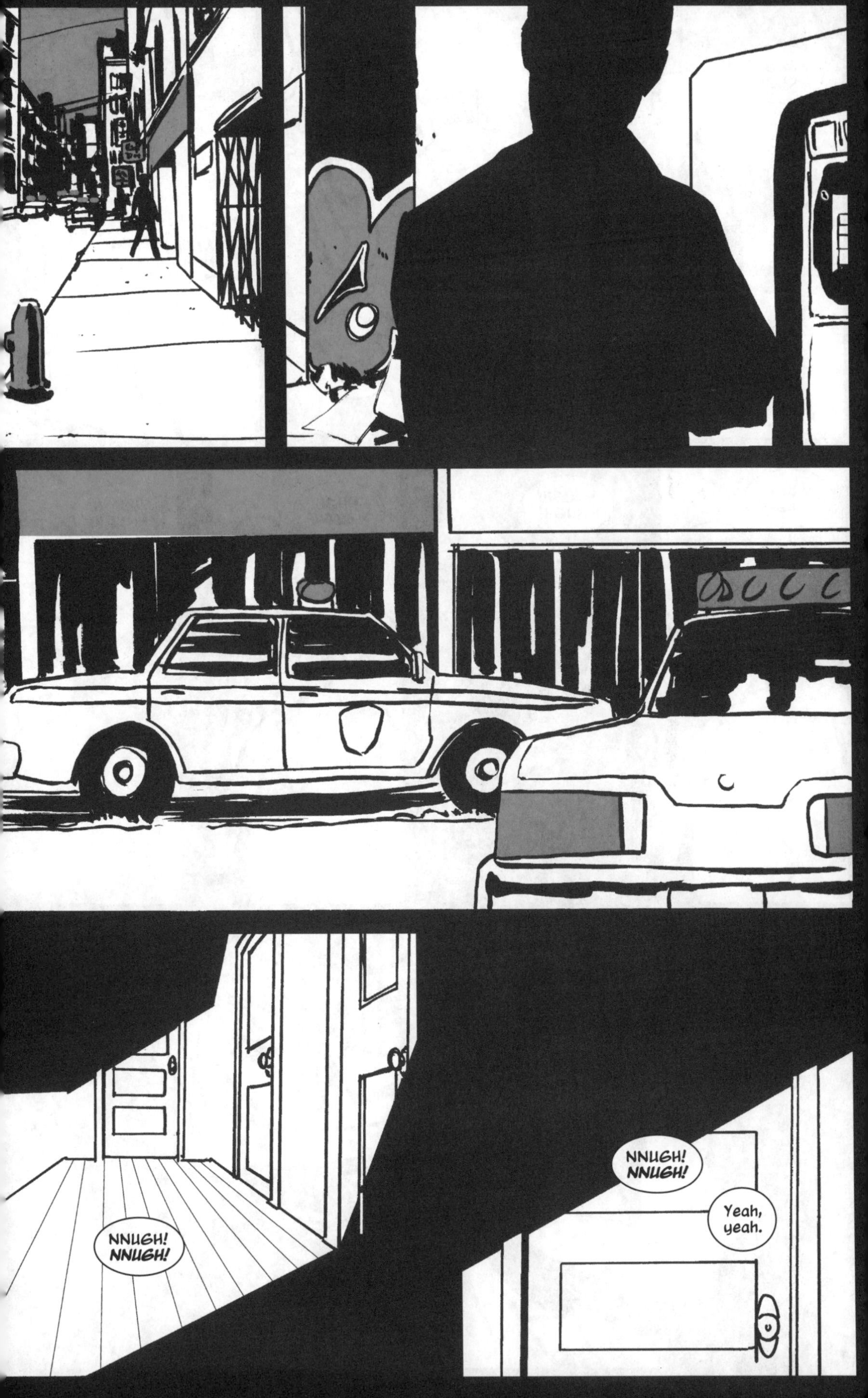
NNUGH!
NNUGH!
NNUGH!
NNUGH!
Yeah, yeah.

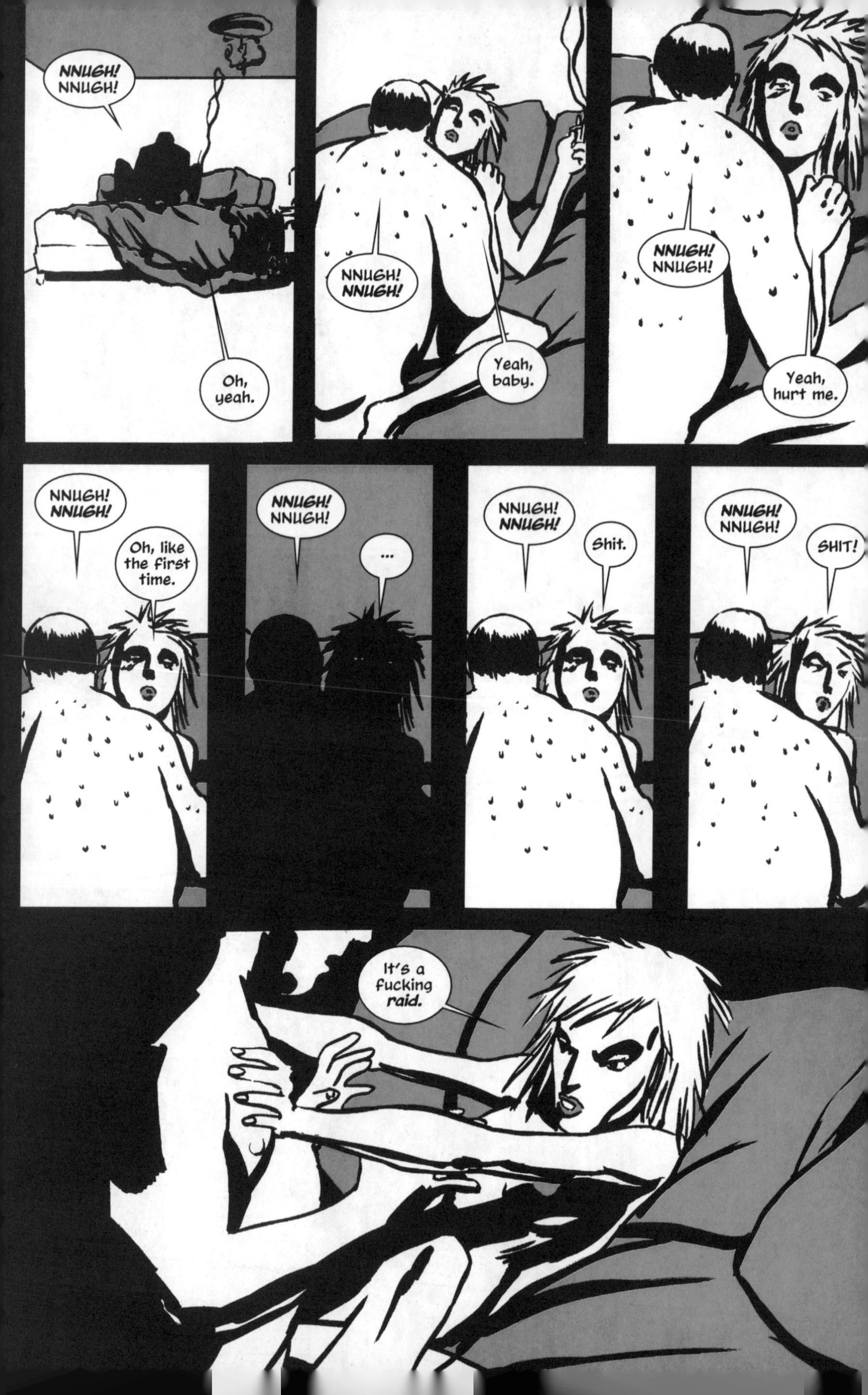
NNUGH! NNUGH!
Oh, yeah.
NNUGH! NNUGH!
Yeah, baby.
NNUGH! NNUGH!
Yeah, hurt me.
NNUGH! NNUGH!
Oh, like the first time.
NNUGH! NNUGH!
...
NNUGH! NNUGH!
Shit.
NNUGH! NNUGH!
SHIT!
It's a fucking raid.

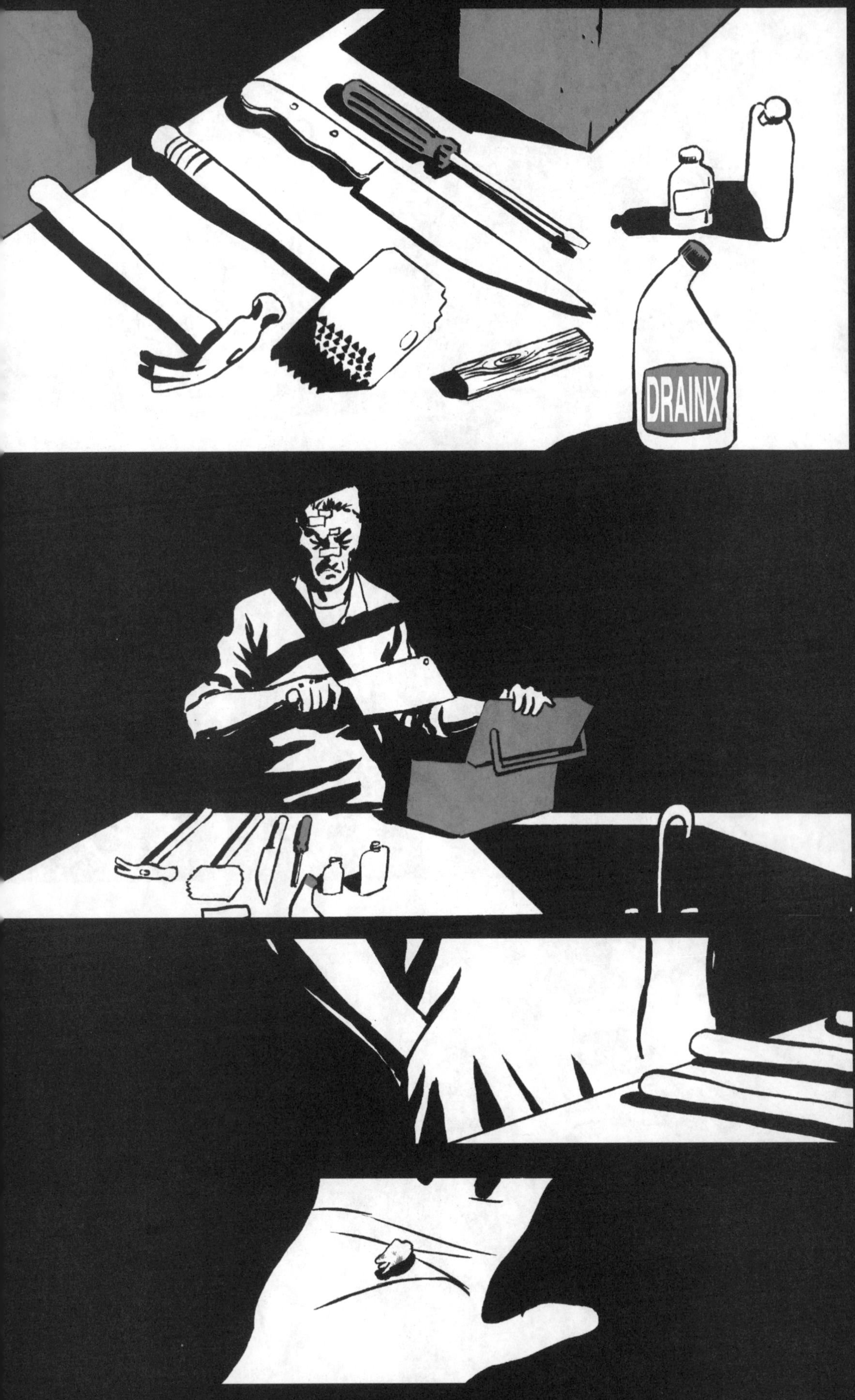
DRAINX

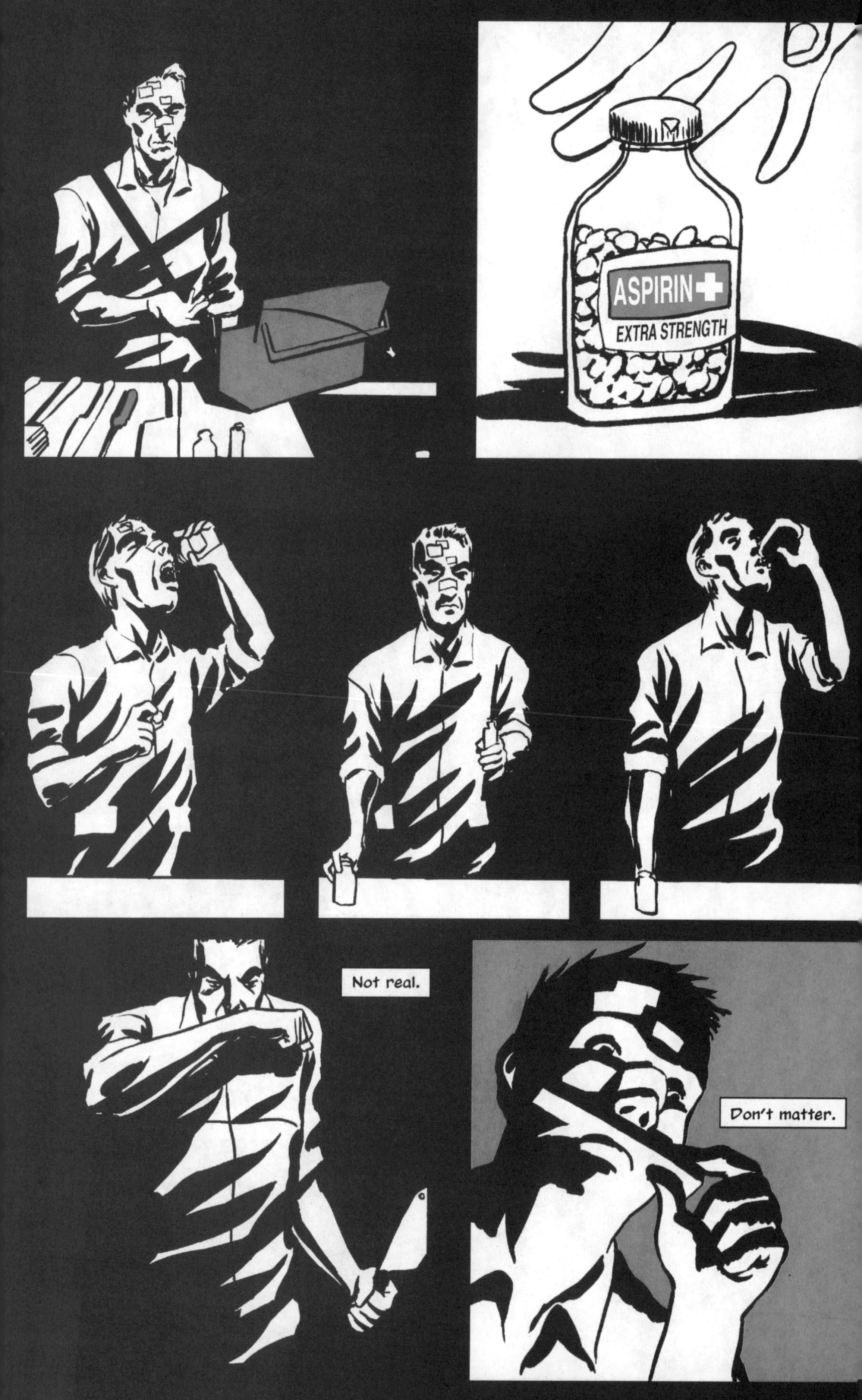
ASPIRIN
EXTRA STRENGTH
Not real.
Don't matter.

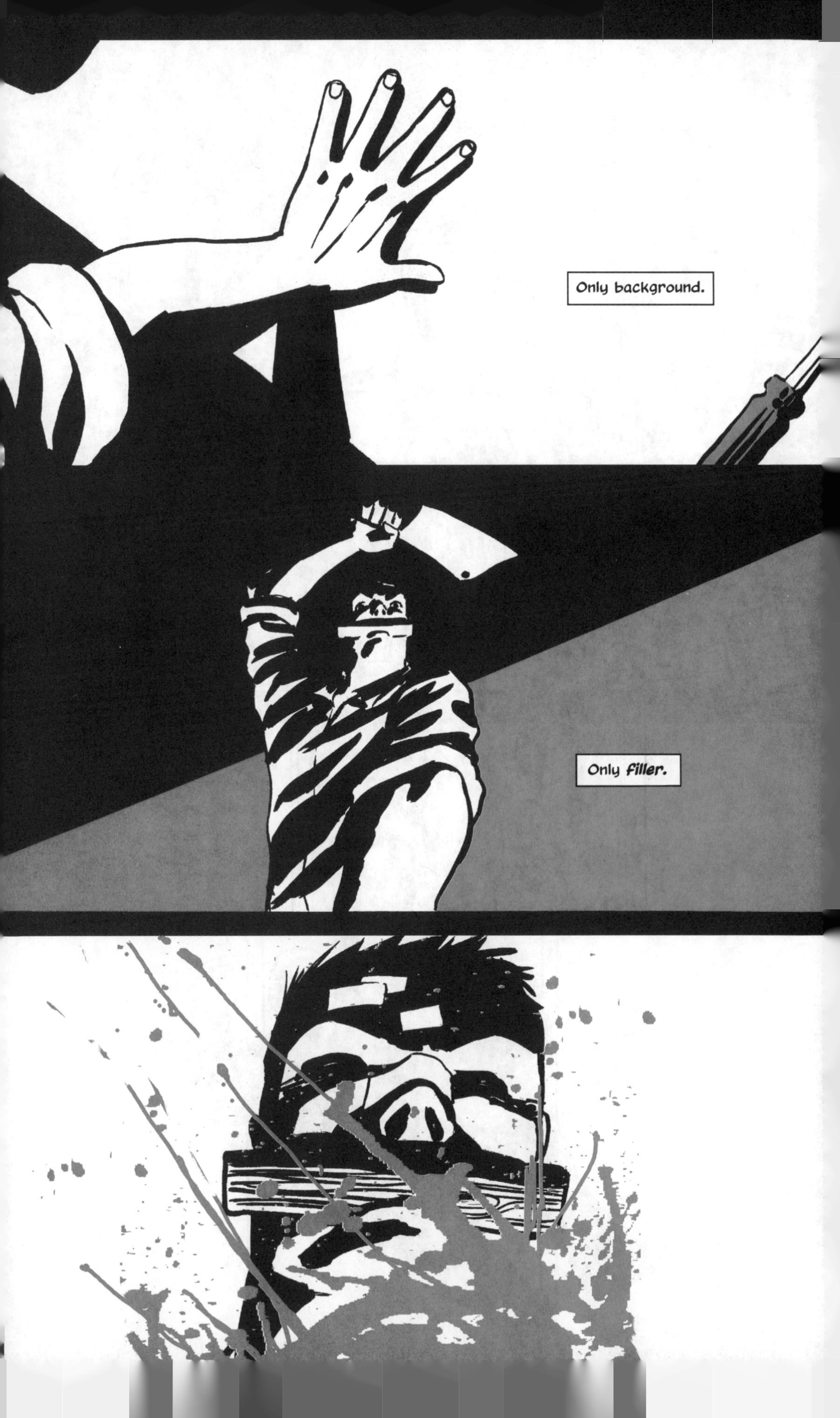
Only background.
Only *filler.*

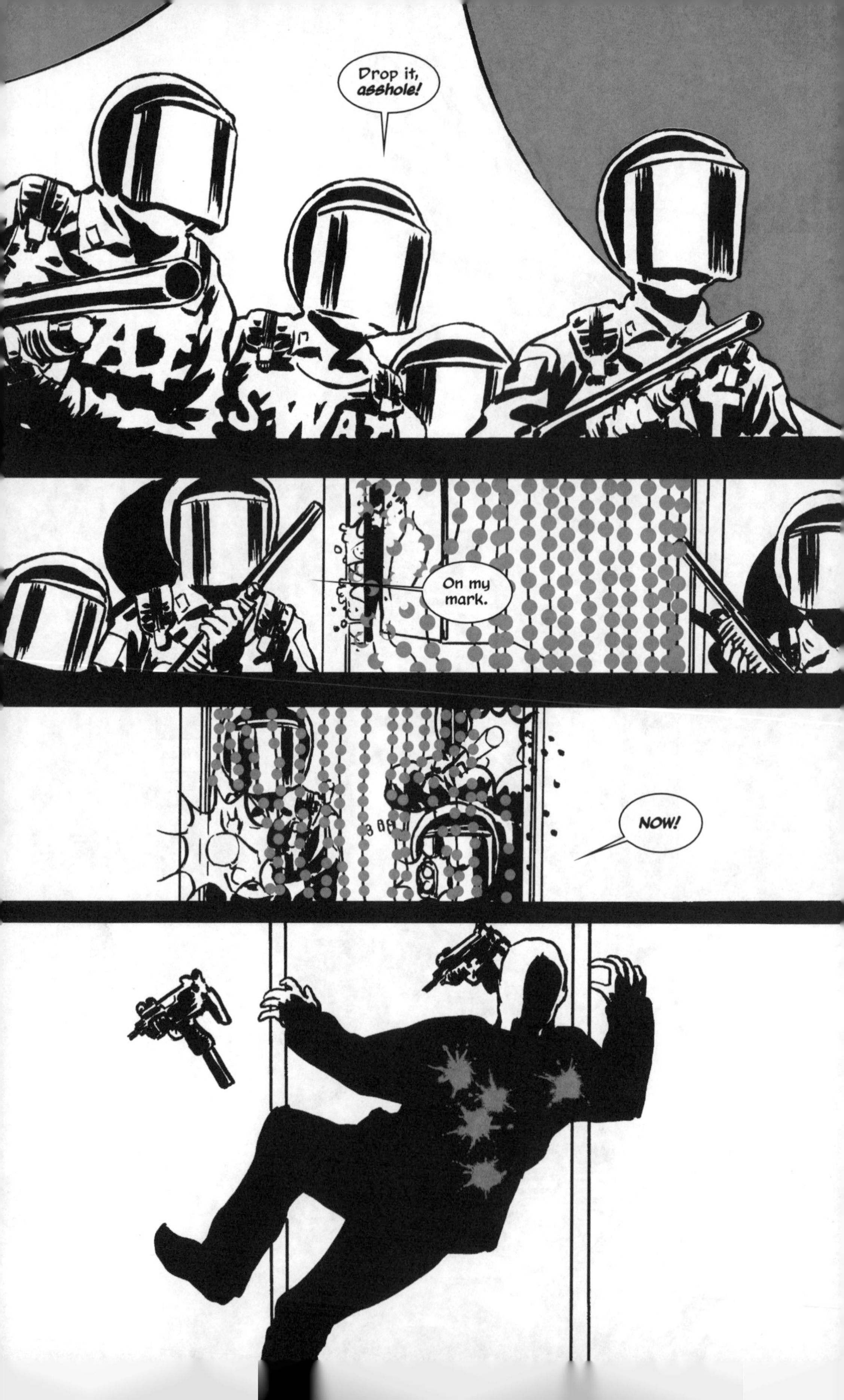
Drop it, asshole!
On my mark.
NOW!

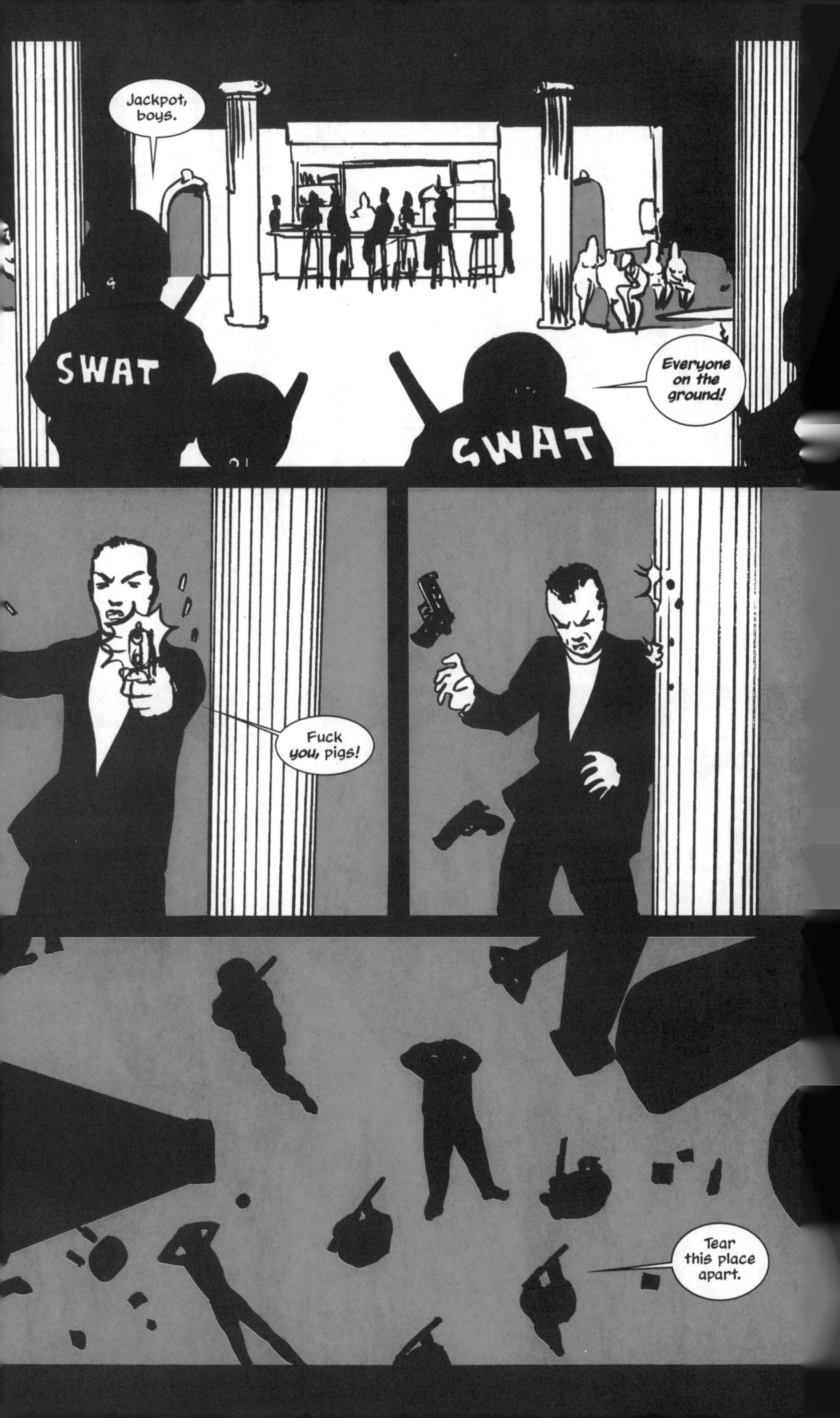
Jackpot, boys.
SWAT
Everyone on the ground!
SWAT
Fuck you, pigs!
Tear this place apart.

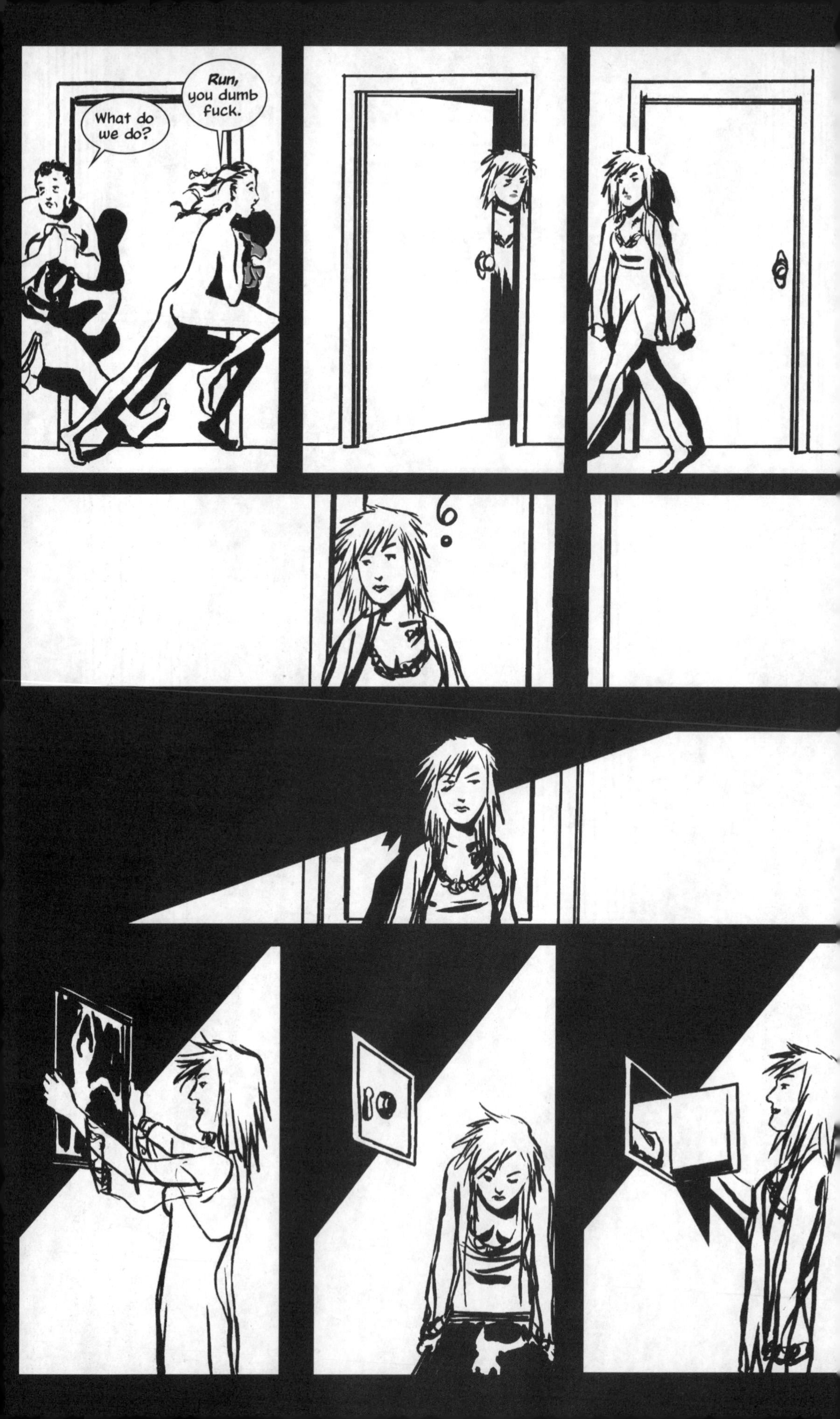
What do we do?
Run, you dumb fuck.

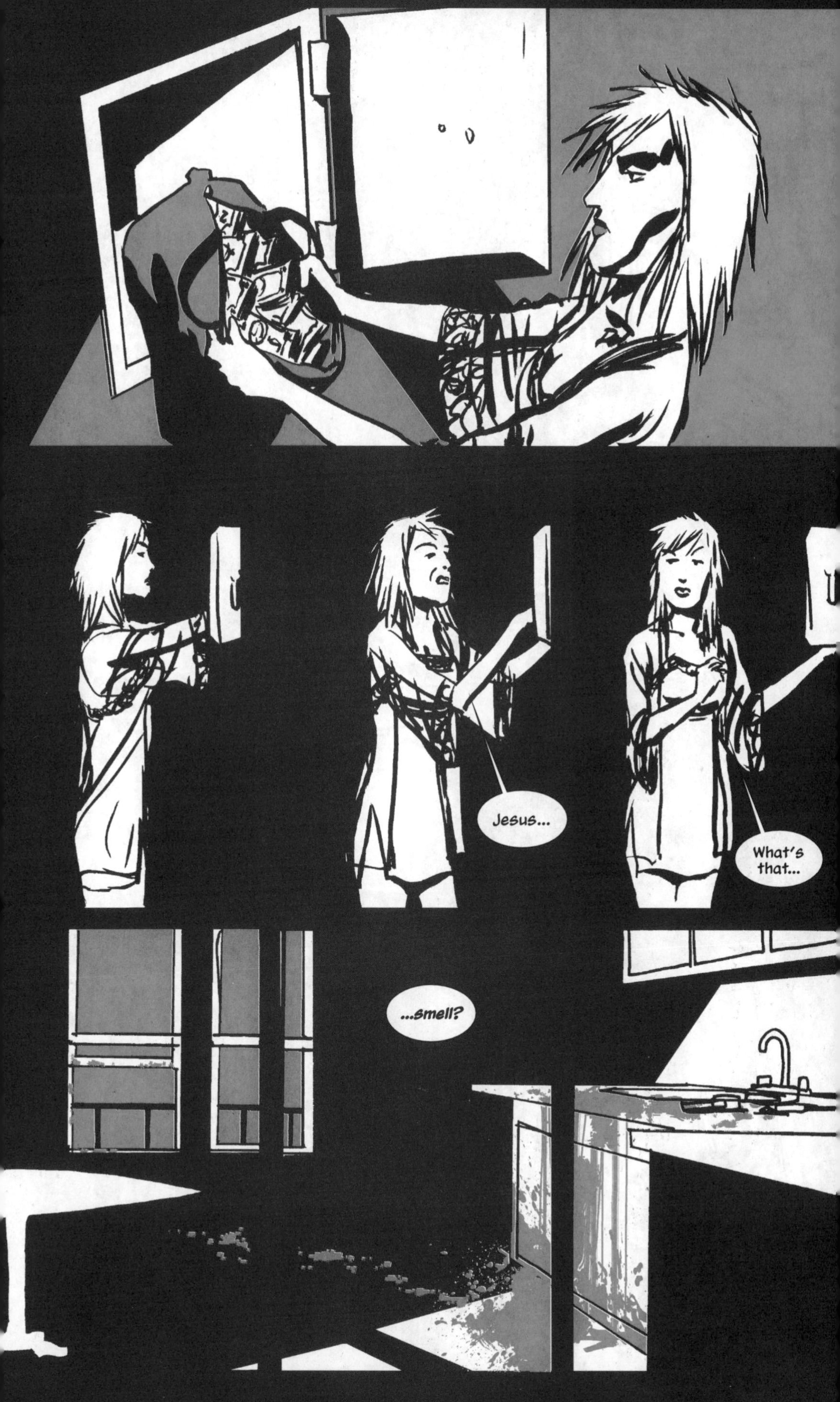
Jesus...
What's that...
...smell?

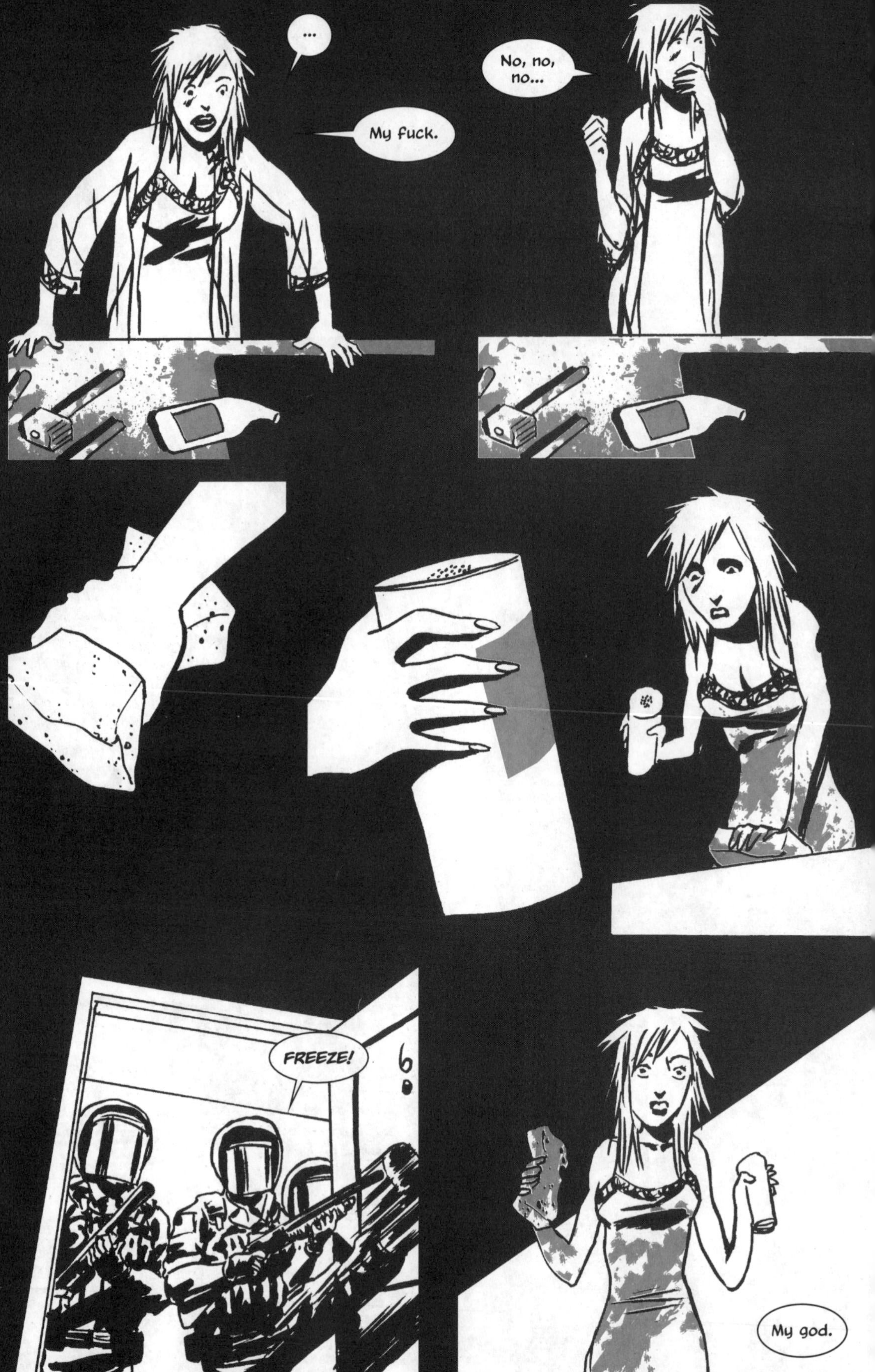
...
My fuck.
No, no, no...
FREEZE!
My god.

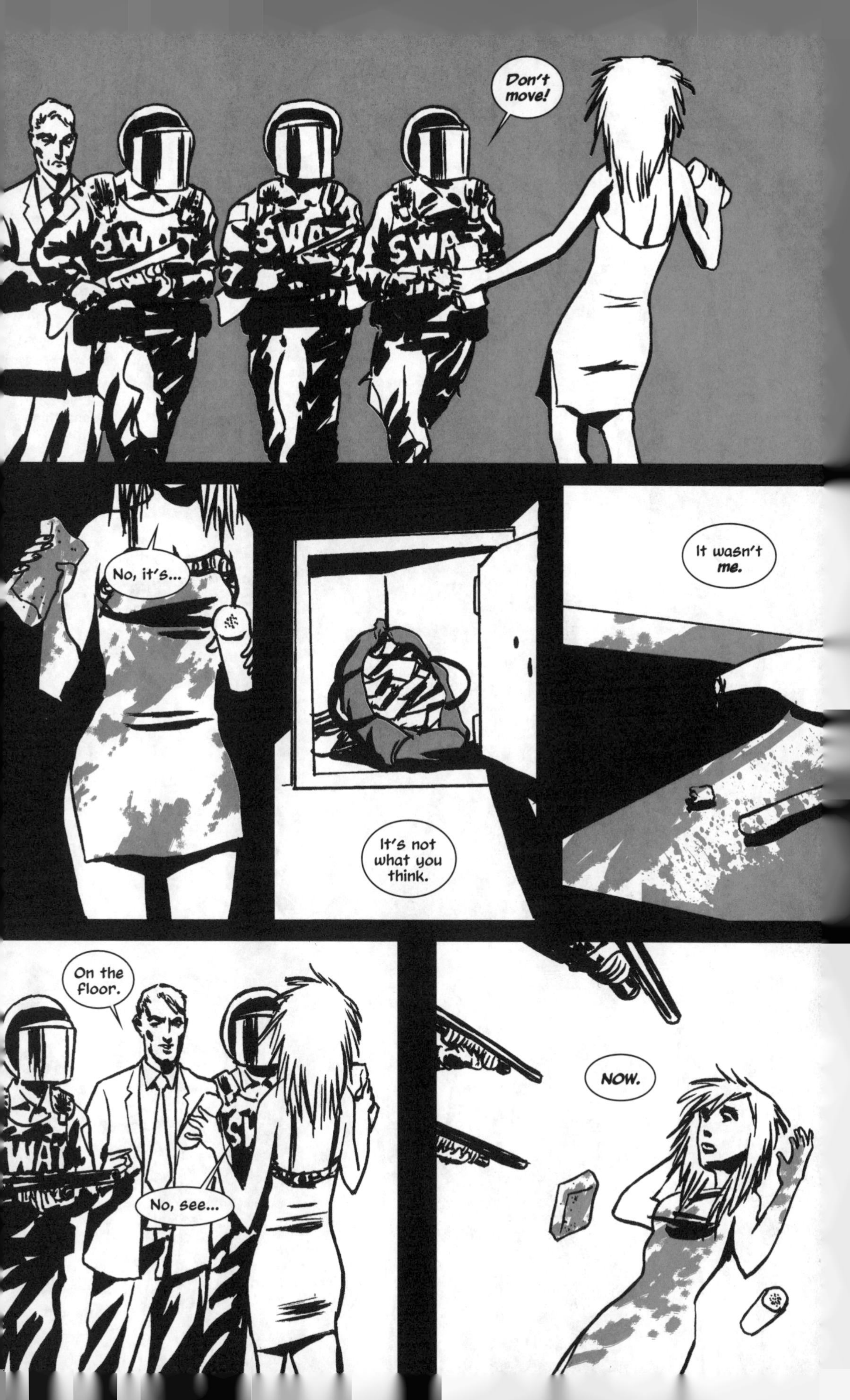
Don't move!
No, it's...
It's not what you think.
It wasn't me.
On the floor.
No, see...
NOW.

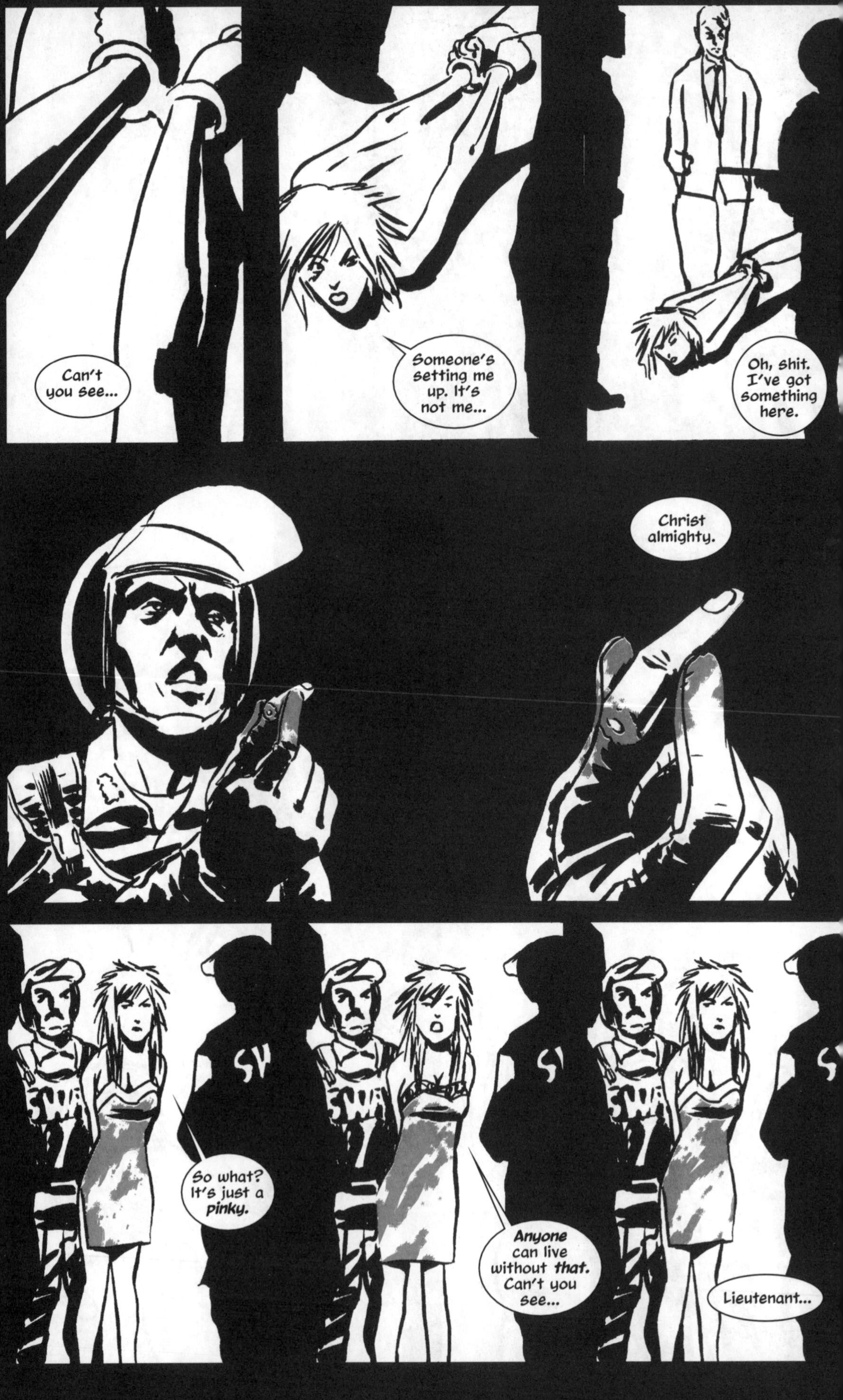
Can't you see...
Someone's setting me up. It's not me...
Oh, shit. I've got something here.
Christ almighty.
So what? It's just a *pinky.*
Anyone can live without *that.* Can't you see...
Lieutenant...

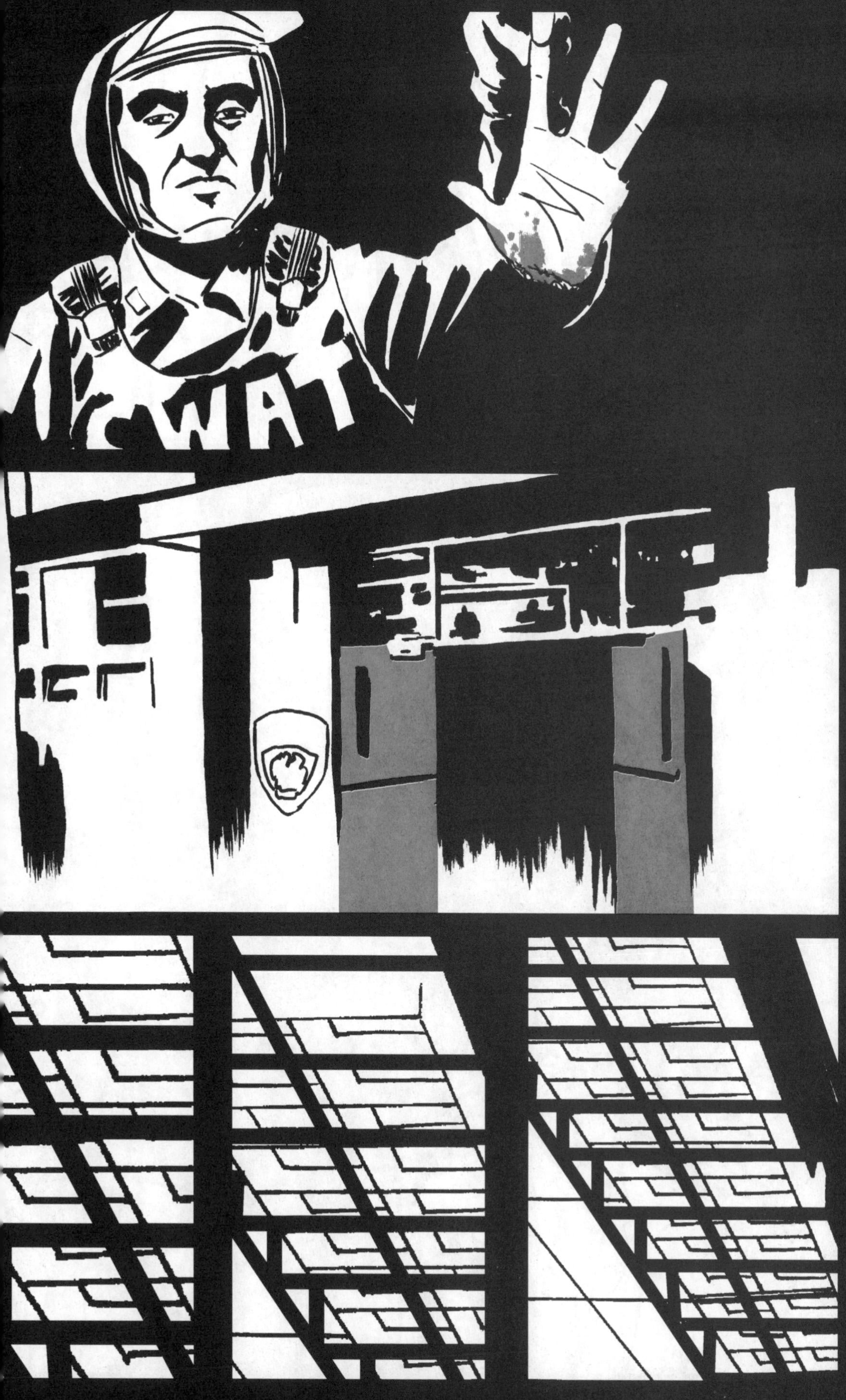
SWAT

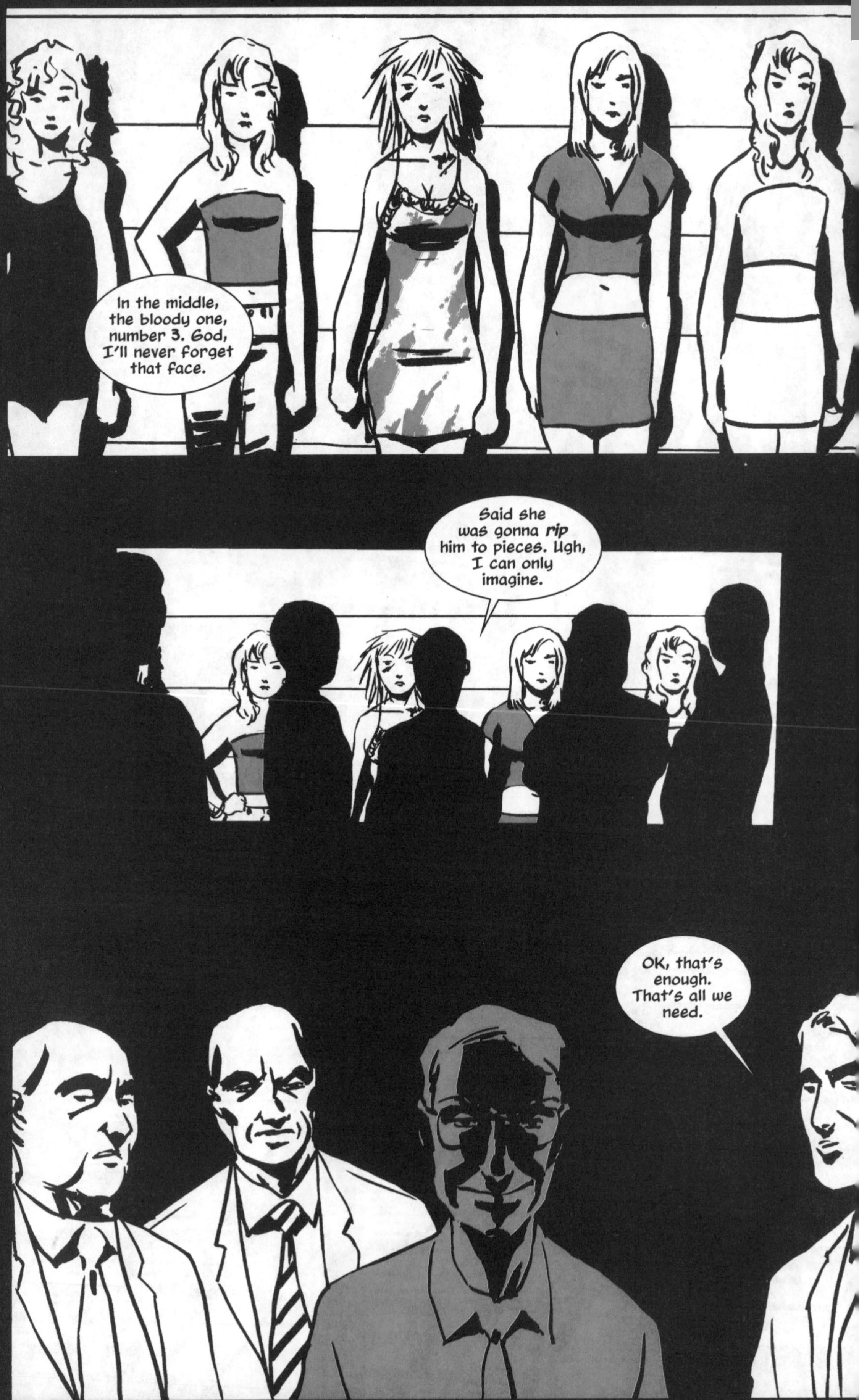
In the middle, the bloody one, number 3. God, I'll never forget that face.
Said she was gonna *rip* him to pieces. Ugh, I can only imagine.
OK, that's enough. That's all we need.

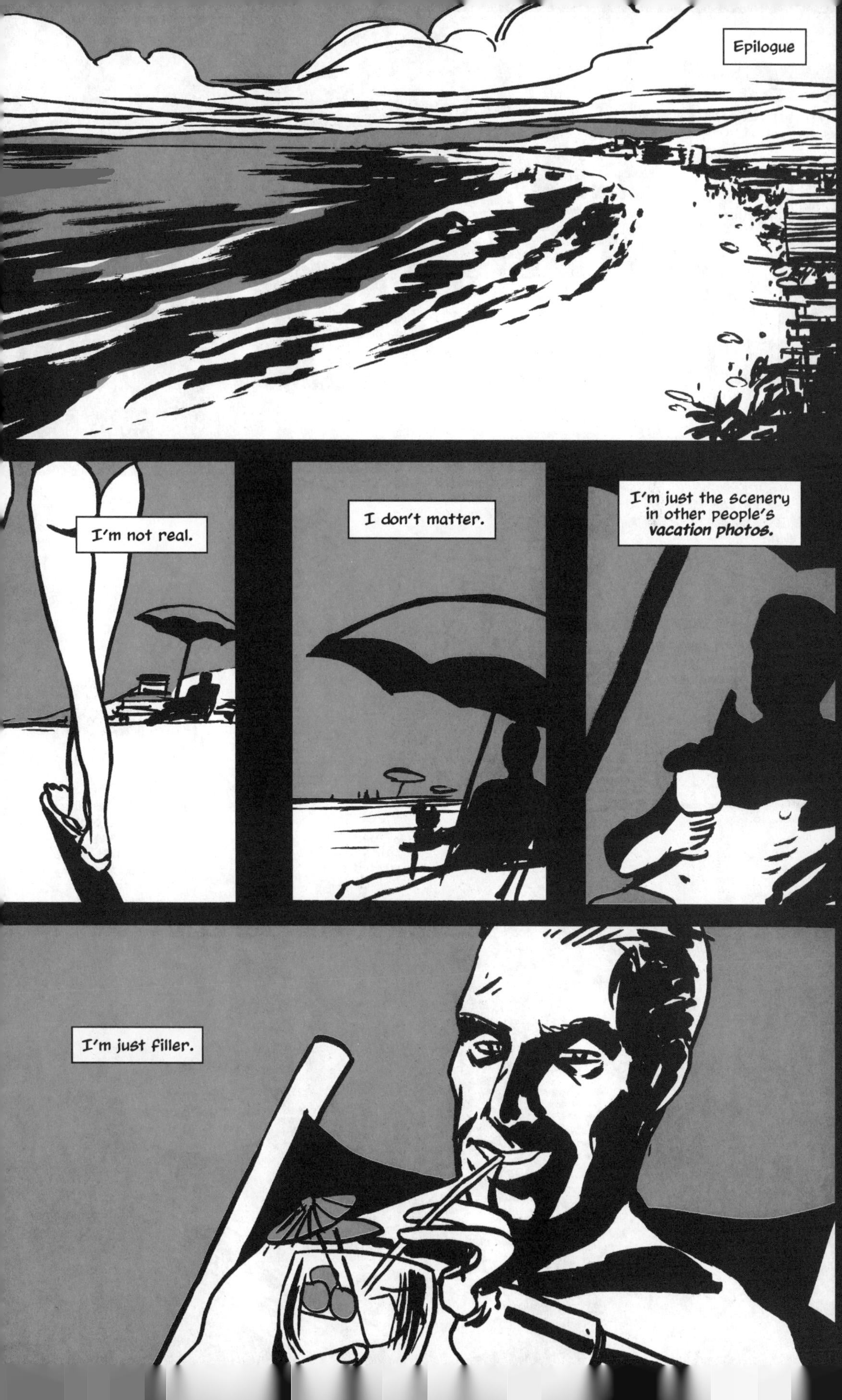
Epilogue
I'm not real.
I don't matter.
I'm just the scenery in other people's *vacation photos.*
I'm just filler.

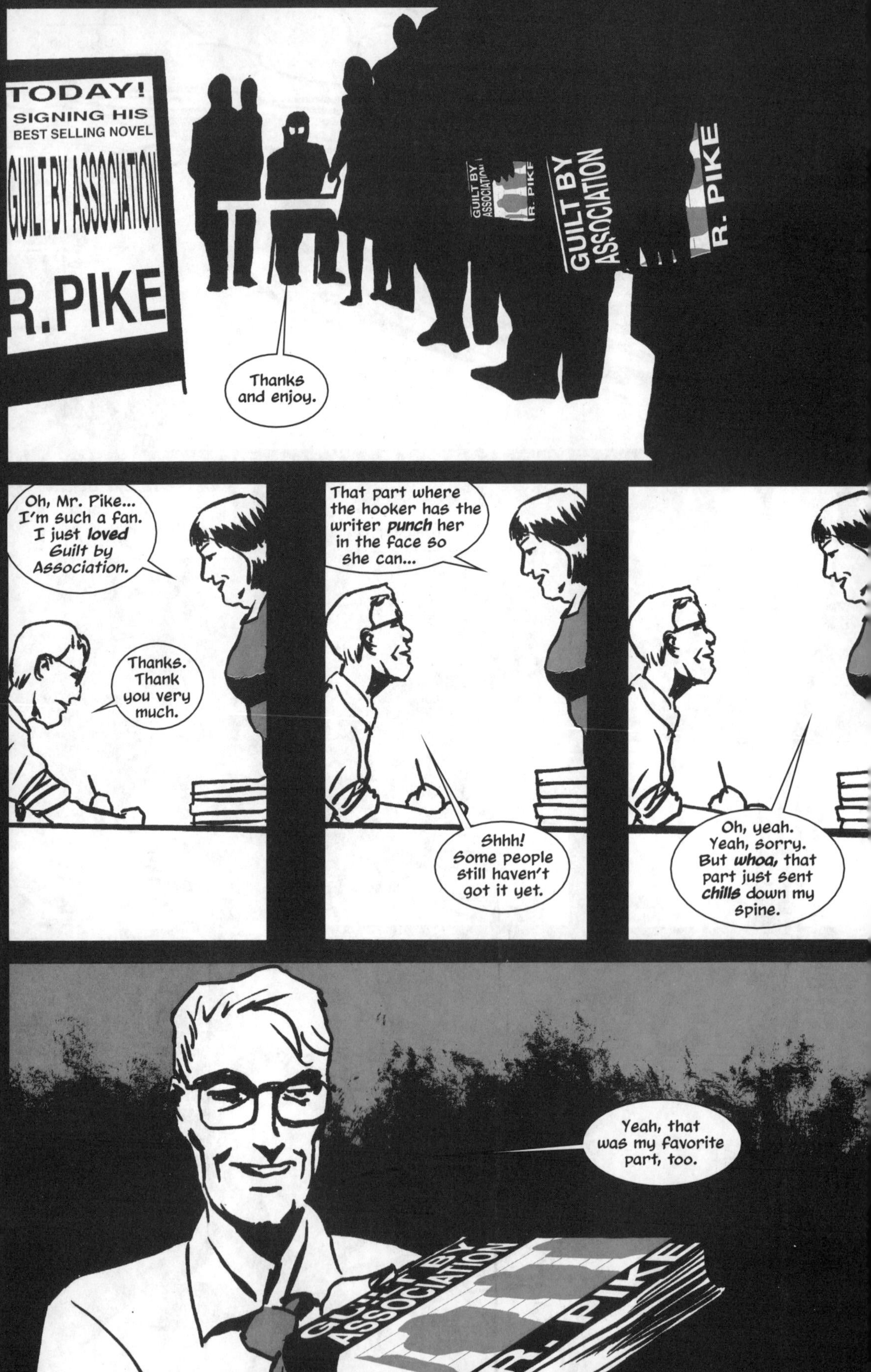
TODAY!
SIGNING HIS
BEST SELLING NOVEL
GUILT BY ASSOCIATION
R.PIKE
GUILT BY ASSOCIATION
R. PIKE
Thanks and enjoy.
Oh, Mr. Pike... I'm such a fan. I just loved Guilt by Association.
Thanks. Thank you very much.
That part where the hooker has the writer punch her in the face so she can...
Shhh! Some people still haven't got it yet.
Oh, yeah. Yeah, sorry. But whoa, that part just sent chills down my spine.
Yeah, that was my favorite part, too.
GUILT BY ASSOCIATION
R. PIKE
THE END